Brad Steiger is the aut[...]
over 15 million copies i[...]
to the inspirational to t[...]
wife in Iowa.

Bizarre Cats, the next in [...] will be published soon by Pan Books.

BRAD STEIGER
BIZARRE CRIME

**A PAN ORIGINAL
PAN BOOKS**
LONDON, SYDNEY AND AUCKLAND

First published 1992 by Signet, an imprint of New American Library,
a division of Penguin Books, USA, Inc.

First published in Great Britain 1993
with additional material by Pan Books Limited
a division of Pan Macmillan Publishers Limited
Cavaye Place London SW10 9PG
and Basingstoke

Associated companies throughout the world

ISBN 0 330 33035 7

Copyright © Brad Steiger, 1992, 1993

The right of Brad Steiger to be identified as the
author of this work has been asserted by him in accordance
with the Copyright, Designs and Patents Act 1988

All rights reserved. No reproduction, copy or transmission
of this publication may be made without written permission.
No paragraph of this publication may be reproduced, copied or
transmitted save with written permission or in accordance with
the provisions of the Copyright Act 1956 (as amended). Any
person who does any authorised act in relation to
this publication may be liable to criminal prosecution
and civil claims for damages

1 3 5 7 9 8 6 4 2

A CIP catalogue record for this book is available from
the British Library

Phototypeset by Intype, London
Printed and bound in Great Britain by
Cox & Wyman Ltd, Reading, Berkshire

This book is sold subject to the condition that it shall not,
by way of trade or otherwise, be lent, re-sold, hired out,
or otherwise circulated without the publisher's prior consent
in any form of binding or cover other than that in which
it is published and without a similar condition including this
condition being imposed on the subsequent purchaser

All of the accounts in this book are completely true reports of actual bizarre crimes, but the names, dates, and places have been changed in order to protect the right of privacy of those whose lives were altered by criminal acts.

Exceptions to this rule are the persons described in the following chapters:

'Dog Is Ordered to Testify in Court Against Burglary Suspect'

'He Provided His Neighbours with Venison, But He Never Shot a Deer in His Life'

'The Great Rejuvenator Who Found the Fountain of Youth'

'Wanted: A Woman to Bear the Child of God!'

'Founder of Weirdo Religion Gives Satan a New Number'

'*Born Free* George Adamson Predicted His Own Murder'

'Who Left the Knife in the Throat of the Seductive Osteopath?'

'He Made a Graveside Vow That He Would Find His Son's Killers'

'Two Angry Disciples Decree: No More Temptations for Jesus'

'Mindreader's Staring Contest with Mass Murderer'

'The Enigma of Charles Manson and His Grisly Family'

'The Quiet Gentleman Who Killed Thirteen in Twelve Minutes'

'The Bible Student Who Believed His "Holy Mission" Was to Strangle Landladies'

'Born to Raise Hell – He Committed One of the Most Brutal Crimes of the Century'

'John Dillinger's $200,000 Five-Hundred-Yard Run'

'The Mystery of Big Jim's Lost Gems'

'The Matriarch of Murder and Mayhem'

'The Beautiful Blonde Angel of Death from Cincinnati'

'The Secret Religious War of a Murderous Mormon Sect'

'Gunmen Place Baby in Microwave Oven to Force Grandfather to Open His Safe'

'The Werewolf of San Francisco'
'Wife of Radio Talk Show Host Kills Herself After Calling in Her Problem'
'Hate-Filled Father Kills Himself, Frames His Son for Murder'
'Three-year-old Placed Under Arrest for Moving Neighbours' Pink Plastic Flamingos.'

CONTENTS

INTRODUCTION
BIZARRE CRIME
xv

CHAPTER ONE
ASSAULT

A Horse Is a Horse, of Course, Unless He Is Also a Police Officer! — 1

Retribution by Lightning Bolt – 'Wrath of God' From the Sky Strikes Wife Beater — 1

CHAPTER TWO
BURGLARY

No Ruler on the Back of the Hand for This Burglar – Nuns in Convent Beat the Devil Out of Intruder — 3

Butcher's Bad Breath Blitzes Burglar — 4

The Painful Dream of a Burglar's Bullet in the Stomach Came True — 5

Trappist Monks Become Holymen From Hell to Thwart Series of Robberies in Their Monastery — 7

In an Incredible Legal Decision – New York Court — 8

Rules That a Person Really Can Be in Two Places at Once

Dog Is Ordered to Testify in Court Against Burglary Suspect — 11

Burglar's Criticism Brought Him to a Dead End — 12

CHAPTER THREE
CANNIBALISM

Satanic Cannibals Terrorize Our State and National Parks — 14

He Provided His Neighbours With Venison but He Never Shot a Deer in His Life — 16

CHAPTER FOUR
DISORDERLY CONDUCT

She Went to Jail for Singing Off Key in the Church Choir — 17

The Big 220 lb Baby Who Crashed Day-Care Centres — 19

It Cost the Lady Tourist a Hefty Fine to Find Out What a Scotsman Wears under His Kilt! — 20

Taught the *ABC*s in Prison, Con Writes Death Threats to Judges — 21

Furious Farmer Blasts Town Hall with Six Tons of Manure — 22

CONTENTS

CHAPTER FIVE
FRAUD

The Living Flame That Sought to Consume London — 24

'Gloat Glands' Brinkley – The Great Rejuvenator Who Found the Fountain of Youth — 29

The Wayward Priest Wanted to Cash in on Judgement Day — 35

Wanted: A Woman to Bear the Child of God – Interested Parties Reply to Jesus and the Mother Spirit — 38

By Displaying Her Webbed Feet, She Proved She Was Not the Corpse in the Grave — 42

CHAPTER SIX
HOMICIDE

A Strange Tale of Two Murdered Irenes — 45

Founder of Weirdo Religion Gives Satan a New Number, Keeps His Girlfriend's Bones in a Bucket — 48

Mother Sued for Fire Damage After Sex Fiend Murders Daughter and Sets Her Ablaze — 50

Three Years in Advance of the Actual Occurrence, *Born Free* George Adamson Predicted His Own Murder — 52

Man Who Killed His Father When He Was Twelve Is Slain by His Own Son Thirty-nine Years Later — 53

Who Left the Knife in the Throat of the Seductive Osteopath?	54
He Always Wanted to Be a Criminal – 'But Not Such a Big One!'	60
He Made a Graveside Vow That He Would Find His Son's Killers	63
The Belch That Cost a Life	64
Two Angry Disciples Decree: No More Temptations for Jesus, as They Blow Him to Kingdom Come With Dynamite	65
Mindreader's Staring Contest With Mass Murderer Produces Hidden Murder Weapon	69

CHAPTER SEVEN
HUMAN SACRIFICE

The Teenagers Chose Jennifer to Be the Sacrificial Lamb on Satan's Altar of Evil	73
They Took a Prostitute From the Streets and Made Her – Mexico's Perverse Priestess of Human Sacrifice	76

CHAPTER EIGHT
KIDNAPPING

Sign This Kid Up to Strike Out Crime! His Bull's-Eye Pitching Helps Nab a Kidnapper	81
Weird Kidnappings and Murders Without Corpses!	83

CONTENTS

CHAPTER NINE
MANSLAUGHTER

Mercy Killer Takes Life of Ailing Uncle, Then Discovers He Did Not Have Fatal Illness — 91

Suspicious Wife Tracking Unfaithful Husband Is Killed When She Tries to Break Into the Wrong House — 92

Violence Begets Violence! Stray Bullet Kills Gunman Who Shot Priest — 93

CHAPTER TEN
MASS MURDER

The Enigma of Charles Manson and His Grisly Family: Why Did They Kill Sharon Tate and Her Friends? — 95

The Quiet Gentleman Who Killed Thirteen in Twelve Minutes — 102

The Bible Student Who Believed His 'Holy Mission' Was to Strangle Landladies — 110

'Born to Raise Hell' – He Committed One of the Most Brutal Crimes of the Century — 115

CHAPTER ELEVEN
MATRICIDE

He Killed His Mother Because She Dated Too Much — 122

Boy Shoots Mum With Hunting Rifle When She Refuses Him a Coca-Cola — 123

CHAPTER TWELVE
MOBSTERS

John Dillinger's $200,000 Five-Hundred-Yard Run — 125

The Mystery of Big Jim's Lost Gems — 128

The Matriarch of Murder and Mayhem Who Became the Crime World's Bloodiest Mama — 131

CHAPTER THIRTEEN
POISONING

The Voodoo Woman's Complaint: 'Everyone I Love Seems to Die!' — 140

The Beautiful Blonde Angel of Death From Cincinnati Who Threw a Farewell Party in Her Prison Death Cell — 144

CHAPTER FOURTEEN
RITUAL MURDERS

The Secret Religious War of a Murderous Mormon Sect — 150

A Weird Unsolved Murder Case – The Bloody Black Magic Deaths of the Healer and His Family — 155

CHAPTER FIFTEEN
ROBBERY

Bandit Is Told He Cannot Complete Holdup Unless He Has an Account at the Bank — 161

CONTENTS

A Sordid Secret Life – Minister Steals Fifty Thousand Dollars to Pay for His Lust for Hookers — 161

At Bit of Heaven Yogurt Shop – Thief Gets Religion Instead of Loot — 162

Gunmen Place Baby in Microwave Oven to Force Grandfather to Open His Safe — 165

Medical School Dropout Heeds Murderous Voices, Robs Banks to Finance Assassinations of Reagan and Bush — 167

Grocery Clerk Foils Armed Robbery by Buying Bandit's Holdup Guns — 170

'Geraldo Made Me Do It!' Couple Rob Bank After Learning How From Talk Show — 172

The Hoodlum Who Invented the 'Mickey Finn' Knockout Drops — 173

Wrinkled, Weathered 'Rambo' Storms London Bank — 175

CHAPTER SIXTEEN
SADISM

The Bloody Bite of Real-Life Vampires — 177

The Werewolf of San Francisco — 184

Man Who Claimed to Be 'Evil Undead' Is Hacked to Pieces by Fearful Vampire Killer — 186

CHAPTER SEVENTEEN
SUICIDE AND SELF-INFLICTED INJURIES

Wife of Radio Talk Show Host Kills Herself After Calling in Her Problem — 192

The Unkindest Crime of All – When Your Right Hand Doesn't Know Your Left Hand Is Strangling You — 193

Fearful of Girlfriend's Wrath, Man Has Himself Shot to Provide Alibi for Being Late — 194

Hate-Filled Father Kills Himself, Frames His Son for Murder — 194

CHAPTER EIGHTEEN
VANDALISM

Three-year-old Placed Under Arrest for Moving Neighbours' Pink Plastic Flamingos — 201

Who Stole the Bones of Edgar Allan Poe? — 204

INTRODUCTION

BIZARRE CRIME

Some of the stories that you will read in this collection of true crimes will strike you as so strange and far-out that you may find yourself laughing out loud and wondering if there truly are any limits to the weird situations in which human beings can place themselves.

We know, of course, that crime of itself should never be considered a laughing matter. Regardless of how humorous a criminal event might seem to an unaffected third party, someone has suffered pain, humiliation, or loss.

Therefore, in the interests of human compassion and good taste, we will refrain from saying that any of the true criminal acts recounted in this book are funny – but there is nothing to prevent us from observing that they are strange, bizarre, paradoxical, ironic, eerie, spooky, and downright weird.

You are about to encounter true tales that run the gamut of the grisly, the gruesome, and the ghoulish. You will read about acts of slashings, stabbings, shootings, and stranglings; deeds of sham, scam and deceit; depraved occurrences of vampirism, cannibalism, human sacrifice, and mass murder. And in each case, the emphasis will be on the strange and off-beat aspects of the crime.

For example, if you were a police officer or a judge, what would you do with the lady who was arrested for robbing two branches of a Florida bank when she insists that she is really seven different people?

In 1980, she actually beat a murder rap on the grounds that the killing was done by one of the other six personalities that inhabit her body. She was committed to a mental institution but given a conditional release in 1987.

Three years later, in 1990, she insisted from her jail cell that one of her other six personalities robbed those banks.

Pretty weird, eh?

Sometimes a victim's narrow escape makes for a bizarre crime story as well. Oliver Anthony of Memphis would never have believed that a fellow could get mugged on a golf course, but a thug walked up to him on the fairway with a pistol in hand and demanded his wallet.

The sixty-one-year-old Anthony decided to resist. It just didn't set well with him to be robbed during his golf game.

His assailant turned to run away, but as he did he fired his pistol at the enraged golfer. It wasn't until Oliver Anthony got back to the clubhouse that he found a bullet embedded in a golf ball in his pocket.

Raymond Meurim of Alberta, Canada, had one of those strange, true 'Bible over heart stops bullet' experiences, too. He took Karl Malden's televised advice never to leave home without traveller's cheques, and he could not have been happier that he did.

While he was visiting Phoenix, Arizona, Raymond was shot by a bandit. The bullet headed straight for his heart, but a batch of traveller's cheques in a shirt pocket deflected the slug, leaving the Canadian with only a couple of bruised ribs.

And we all love stories about incredible coincidences.

While Sandra Rock of Grand Island, Nebraska, was visiting her daughter Kimberly, a cashier in an Omaha supermarket, she had five hundred dollars in traveller's cheques stolen from her.

Some time later during Mrs Rock's stay in Omaha, a

woman entered the market where Kimberly worked, showed identification, then presented traveller's cheques to be cashed. They all had Sandra Rock's signature on them. Kimberly promptly notified the police, and the woman was arrested.

Bizarre Crime also deals with accounts of how psychics solved murders and kidnappings, and how ordinary people's frightening dreams of the future actually came true.

In April 1974, Lyne Rogers, a young woman from Seattle, dreamed four nights in a row that she would be raped in the downtown city library.

One night in July, as she browsed in the city library searching for a particular book on Beethoven, she noticed a man staring at her. Then, quite obviously, he began to follow her.

To Lyne's horror, he followed her into the women's washroom, seized her from behind, and told her that he would knife her if she screamed or resisted.

As he reached for a piece of rope with which to bind her, she did as she had done in her dreams: she kicked him in the groin.

Although she fainted after she had delivered the blow with all her strength, it hit home. The would-be rapist hobbled out of the ladies' room bent over in pain – and disappeared.

Neither can we neglect stories of real vampires, werewolves, and cannibals – true accounts of men and women who have transformed themselves quite literally into creatures of darkness.

There is the sad tale of a man who was so convincing in his claims that he was one of the 'evil undead' that he got himself hacked to bits.

Marty Hughes of South Carolina suffered from a rare blood disease that caused him to joke that he was really a vampire. The fact that he was obsessed by the occult and boasted that he could work black magic certainly added to his sinister mystique. Marty became so convincing to fearful vampire killer Dean Bolan that Bolan protected himself by chopping Marty into tiny pieces.

Bizarre Crime is divided into eighteen chapters of bizarre, strange, and sometimes wacky criminal acts. There is certain to be something here to confound or to shock even the most jaded of connoisseurs of the weird, the wild, and the wicked.

Brad Steiger
Cave Creek, Arizona
March 1991

CHAPTER ONE

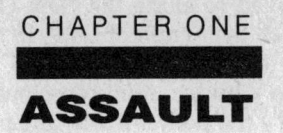

ASSAULT

A HORSE IS A HORSE, OF COURSE, UNLESS HE IS ALSO A POLICE OFFICER!

In December 1990, a Florida judge informed Moses Jefferson that a horse is not always just a horse – sometimes a horse must be defined as a very large cop.

Jefferson was sentenced to one year in prison for assaulting a police officer when he was found guilty of kicking Majestic Warrior, Officer M. P. Brown's horse. Officer Brown had been attempting to arrest Jefferson for failure to appear in court when he kicked the horse twice in the thigh. The horse reared in protest at the sudden abuse, but it wasn't seriously hurt.

The judge said that he could not condone an assault on a police officer by an attack on his horse. Jefferson had created a threat to others as evidenced by his hauling off and kicking the horse.

RETRIBUTION BY LIGHTNING BOLT – 'WRATH OF GOD' FROM THE SKY STRIKES WIFE BEATER

Sadly, alleged wife beater Bernie Sharkey truly permitted his inner demons to gain control of his terrible temper on 27 April 1991, when he stabbed his wife Josie in the back and in the throat.

Sharkey managed to elude the New Orleans police for two days, but then the 'wrath of God', in the form of a bolt out of the blue, struck him down. Two fishermen found him collapsed on a bridge, semi-conscious, mumbling that he was wanted by the police. It was apparent that the wife beater had been able to duck the cops but couldn't escape the 'hand of God'.

A police spokesperson stated that Bernie Sharkey had been struck by lightning while crossing a bridge. Lightning had hit his hand, shot through his entire body, and come out of his foot.

'Maybe the police couldn't get him,' the spokesperson commented, 'but God sure did. There is no doubt that Sharkey thought that he had felt the wrath of God.'

An additional bit of irony to the case developed when Sharkey was taken to the same hospital where, two days before, paramedics had rushed his thirty-year-old wife after he had stabbed her and fled.

Sharkey recovered from the ultimate shock treatment, and his wife survived the stab wounds. He was charged with aggravated battery and parole violation and released on bail with a restraining order to stay away from his wife.

It is unlikely that he will bother her again, since Bernie Sharkey should fear that lightning could strike twice.

CHAPTER TWO

BURGLARY

NO RULER ON THE BACK OF THE HAND FOR THIS BURGLAR – NUNS IN CONVENT BEAT THE DEVIL OUT OF INTRUDER

When husky, 240 lb Ruben Castanos decided to break into the quiet convent in Baltimore, Maryland, on 28 January, 1989, he thought the burglary would be a piece of cake. But when six nuns finished with him, the police had to take him to the hospital with loosened teeth, cuts, and bruises.

Sister Maria heard the telltale sounds of forced entry about 3:00 a.m. There was a noise at the back door, followed by a shattering of glass.

Sister Maria ran out into the hall and telephoned the police. Once she had informed the station house that someone was breaking into the convent, she shouted an alarm to the other sisters.

Before she had cradled the telephone receiver, Castanos suddenly appeared before her and ordered her to drop the phone and to lie down on the floor. When Sister Maria refused, the burglar punched her on the nose.

Stunned by the vicious blow, Sister Maria nevertheless stood her ground and refused to drop the telephone receiver. She was determined that this intruder would not steal what few possessions they had in the convent.

About this time, reinforcements arrived in the persons of five other sisters who had emerged from their rooms. Two of them held Castanos' arms, and the three others began punching him anywhere they could reach his body or his face. The sisters continued pummelling the burglar until they had him pinned against the wall.

Having had enough of such punishment, Castanos managed to break free, and he sent seventy-six-year-old Sister Beatriz spinning to the floor. Fortunately, the elderly nun was not seriously harmed by the burly burglar's stiff-arm tactics.

Slamming open the door to the convent, Castanos was glad to be free of the fighting nuns. His freedom was short lived, however, for he ran straight into the arms of the police.

Sergeant William Dillard of the Baltimore Police Department agreed with the battered burglar that he had definitely chosen the wrong place to break into when he broke into the convent. 'Castanos got more than he bargained for, that's for sure!'

He was sent to jail to await trial on five charges, including burglary and assault.

BUTCHER'S BAD BREATH BLITZES BURGLAR

In his neighbourhood in northern Sicily, the breath of Anthony Mariano, the friendly butcher, is legendary. No one, they say, has ever had breath so bad, so foul, so wretched as Anthony's.

Anthony has no trouble with his teeth nor does he suffer from any digestive problem. He is simply a robust butcher who enjoys sampling his own wares. He passionately loves strong, aged cheeses, and he munches on strong, spicy salami all day long.

His wife Ramona is the first to testify that even though Anthony does brush his teeth regularly, no amount of brushing with any known brand of toothpaste can sweeten his breath.

As weird as it may seem, Anthony's bad breath proved to be his most effective weapon when he encountered a burglar in his home in September 1989.

Dom Baliti, twenty-seven, had only recently arrived in the city to ply his craft as a burglar. As fate would have it, he chose the Mariano home for his initial heist.

As he was creeping silently up the stairs, a creaking step board betrayed his alien presence in the Mariano home. Anthony, forty-two, stepped from his bedroom to investigate and surprised Dom on the stairs.

Quickly concluding that it was time to flee, Dom sought to make good his getaway by punching Anthony in the stomach. The sudden, unexpected blow knocked the wind out of the butcher, but with the expelled blast of breath from Anthony's innards came an odour so powerful and so foul that Baliti began to gag. While the burglar gasped from the gas attack, the butcher recovered from the surprise blow and regained enough equilibrium to let the thief have it with a solid punch to the nose.

Baliti was still lying on the floor moaning when the police arrived.

Ramona shrugged that she had grown used to her husband's bad breath, but she could understand how many people would find it offensive.

As for Anthony, well, he was never really embarrassed about his foul breath before, but, now, according to Ramona, 'He is proud of how bad it smells. He brags that it probably saved his life.'

THE PAINFUL DREAM OF A BURGLAR'S BULLET IN THE STOMACH CAME TRUE

On 6 May 1971, Mrs Agnes Toutin, aged fifty, was having a restless night. As she tossed and turned, a dream began to play before her mind. Then, suddenly, with a scream of terror, she bolted upright in bed.

'I dreamed that a stranger was in our house and that he shot me in the stomach,' she told her startled husband, William.

Toutin calmed his wife with the usual mumbled assurances that her nightmare was only a dream, nothing to worry about. Somewhat mollified, but still frightened, Mrs Toutin managed to fall into fitful slumber.

The next morning, Mrs Toutin, who lived in Glanford Township, Ontario, told her frightening dream to her neighbour, Mrs Hilda Foote. After their visit, Agnes Toutin returned to her home, resolving to put the nightmare from her mind.

That afternoon, she was upstairs getting some material to cover a chair when she heard a strange noise in the living room. Coming downstairs, she surprised a burglar in the act of ransacking her house.

Pointing a pistol menacingly in her direction, the man demanded money. When Mrs Toutin protested that she had none, the burglar cocked the pistol and fired into her stomach.

After the man had fled, she managed to crawl to the telephone and place a call to her neighbour, Mrs Foote. Hilda Foote telephoned her husband, Harvey, and he called an ambulance. Mrs Toutin was declared to be in satisfactory condition after two hours of surgery.

'Agnes told me at 10:00 a.m. that she dreamed last night that a stranger would shoot her in the stomach,' Mrs Foote commented. 'It's real strange. The good Lord usually doesn't let you know what's going to happen to you.'

TRAPPIST MONKS BECOME HOLYMEN FROM HELL TO THWART SERIES OF ROBBERIES IN THEIR MONASTERY

The wealthy, isolated monastery of Notre-Dame des Neiges near Saint-Laurent-les-Bains, France, had already been hit twice by gangs of thieves in 1990. Revd Pierre-Marie, abbot of the nineteenth-century Trappist monastery, knew that the besieged monks must heed their belief that God helps those who help themselves. In previous robberies, the telephone lines had been cut so that the monks could not even call for help. It was now time to organize their own forces of self-defence.

The monastery, located in southern France's Languedoc region, produces four million bottles of fine wine each year on its immense estate. Although the monastery of Notre-Dame des Neiges is occupied by thirty-six Trappist monks who live existences set apart from the world, the sale of the wine none the less produces a great deal of money, which tempts burglars and thieves attracted by visions of cash stashed in darkened corners of the monastery.

On 6 November 1990, a burglar alarm sounded at 3:00 a.m., an hour before the monks would have been at morning prayers. The alerted Trappists jumped out of their beds, armed themselves with shot-guns, and marched outside to meet the invaders.

A police spokesman determined later that one of the brothers fired a blast into the air, flushing out two masked men who were hiding in some bushes. The thieves, spotting the monkish militia heading towards them, decided to retreat down the road leading from the monastery.

The bandits next found that the car that awaited them in their escape route had been blocked by a parked car and by a shot-gun wielding monk who demanded that they stop. The two accomplices of the thieves opened fire on the brave Brother Zepherin with a shot-gun and a semi-automatic pistol, and he went down with two hundred shot-gun pellets in his leg.

Other monks in their own cars closed in on the four men and returned the bandits' fire with roaring volleys of shot-gun blasts. The would-be thieves managed to escape, but they were forced to flee empty handed.

'Now that the Trappist Brothers have armed themselves and have shown themselves quite capable of defending the monastery against the assault of thieves, it seems very unlikely that burglars will be so eager to try to break in and steal from them,' a police spokesman commented.

IN AN INCREDIBLE LEGAL DECISION – NEW YORK COURT RULES THAT A PERSON REALLY CAN BE IN TWO PLACES AT ONCE

On 8 July 1896, a perplexed William MacDonald sat in a New York City courtroom and heard himself formally accused of attempting to burglarize an apartment house on Second Avenue. According to several witnesses, MacDonald had been discovered bumping about in a room, apparently attempting to make off with valuable items.

Some of the witnesses had tried to grab the thief, but he had somehow managed to escape. All of the witnesses testified, however, that they had had the opportunity for a good look at him.

When the baffled William MacDonald was arrested by the police and taken before the witnesses, they were unanimous in swearing that he was definitely the man they had seen in the house on Second Avenue.

Although MacDonald could offer little by way of an alibi without the testimony of a certain corroborating witness, his attorney found that this key witness was most willing to appear on the accused man's behalf. The witness was Professor Wein, a noted New York hypnotist who enjoyed a solid reputation in the world of conventional, scientific medicine.

'On the very hour in which Mr William MacDonald is accused of attempting to burgle the house on Second Avenue,' Professor Wein told an astonished courtroom, 'he was in reality on the stage of a Brooklyn vaudeville house, which is more than five miles away from the aforementioned apartment house.

'What is more,' Professor Wein continued, his voice rising above the doubtful and puzzled whispers, 'Mr MacDonald was under the close scrutiny of an audience of several hundred people. You see, he was assisting me in my performance, and I had placed him in a deep hypnotic trance.'

The judge frowned and rapped his gavel for silence as excited murmurs arose from spectators and jury members alike. The prosecuting attorney seemed stunned by such a preposterous pronouncement.

But the time for incredible courtroom revelation had only just begun.

With the permission of the court, MacDonald's attorney called ten reputable Brooklyn residents before the judge's bench. Professor Wein explained that these men and women had served as a committee on the stage while he was performing. It had been their function to see that his claims for hypnosis were not implemented in any way by any sort of trickery. Now, matters of a serious nature had arisen that would permit the members of the committee to serve quite another purpose: they could identify William MacDonald as the man Professor Wein had placed in a deep trance.

The prosecuting attorney sat very still for a few moments after the defence attorney indicated that he might cross-examine the hypnotist. He had walked into the courtroom with what had seemed to be an open-and-shut case of a man clearly seen while attempting a burglary. Now, in the most remarkable way imaginable, his task had been made much more difficult.

The prosecutor had to ask Professor Wein the obvious question: 'Do you mean to tell the court that it was possible for William MacDonald to be in two places at the same time?'

'What I mean to tell the court,' Professor Wein answered without hesitation, 'is that the *physical* William MacDonald never left the stage of the Brooklyn vaudeville house. The residents of the apartment house on Second Avenue may have seen a non-physical image of Mr MacDonald.'

'Am I to understand,' the prosecutor pressed on, 'that you believe it to be possible for MacDonald's spirit to wander about while his physical body was on the stage of the theatre?'

Professor Wein acknowledged his belief that such a phenomenon was quite possible.

While the judge once again sounded his gavel to call for silence in the courtroom, the prosecutor scratched his chin reflectively, then continued his cross-examination. 'What did you suggest that MacDonald *do* while under your hypnotic trance?'

Professor Wein explained that he had only placed MacDonald in a deep sleep. He was firm on the point that he had not suggested that his hypnotic subject 'travel' to New York. Nor had the hypnotist even thought of New York during the demonstration.

'Was it a part of your demonstration, your performance, to command Mr MacDonald to commit a crime or to act out the perpetration of a crime?' the prosecutor asked pointedly.

The professor answered sharply that such had not been the case.

The prosecutor paused in his questioning, as if expecting the defence attorney to object to his line of examination. No objection came. The defence was allowing Professor Wein's testimony to establish its case, and it had no fear that the prosecutor might be able to trip him up.

'Is Mr MacDonald a good subject?' he asked, breaking his silence.

Professor Wein stated that he was one of the best hypnotic subjects that he had ever encountered. 'I am convinced that Mr MacDonald, while in the hypnotic state, would carry out all of my suggestions with certain limits. I must stress, however, that I would never suggest that any subject commit or dramatize the perpetration of any criminal act. I consider that my subjects are deprived for a certain time of all sensations other than those which I impose upon them. Such an out-of-body experience as that which Mr MacDonald underwent is not without precedent in the annals of hypnosis.'

Although the prosecuting attorney did his best to undermine the professor's testimony by attempting to portray such an experience as fantastic and unbelievable, the serious manner of Professor Wein, coupled with the accounts of the ten witnesses who had been present at the vaudeville house on the evening of the demonstration, convinced the jury to return a verdict of 'not guilty' for William MacDonald. For the first time known in the annals of law, a New York jury had placed credence in a case of psychic phenomena and had acquitted a man on the evidence that he had literally been in two places at one time.

DOG IS ORDERED TO TESTIFY IN COURT AGAINST BURGLARY SUSPECT

When Topeka, Kansas, sheriff's deputy Russell Berry arrived to subpoena Officer Bubba to testify against a twenty-year-old suspected burglar, he immediately perceived that someone in the district attorney's office had made a decided error in identification. Amidst howls of laughter, Deputy Berry readily appraised 'Officer Bubba' as a 110 lb German shepherd.

Officer Ray Hester, joining in the deputy's amusement, agreed to transform the weird error into a joke on the DA's office, and he 'signed' the subpoena by drawing a dog's pawprint on it.

Assistant District Attorney Jim Welch good-naturedly admitted that his office had goofed, but he hastened to point out that the error had been committed in the interest of thorough police work and professionalism.

On 23 September 1989, Bubba had assisted in the capture of a burglar inside a Topeka delicatessen. While preparing to prosecute the defendant in May 1990, Welch gave his secretary the file on the case and told her to subpoena all the witnesses.

As a matter of routine, the assistant district attorney said, he always lists all the witnesses in each criminal investigation – even the police dogs – in order to provide the defence attorneys with all the information that they might need to build their case.

When Welch's secretary followed his instructions to the letter and typed up subpoenas for all the officers named in the case, she had no idea that Bubba was a four-legged police officer.

BURGLAR'S CRITICISM BROUGHT HIM TO A DEAD END

On a Friday night in December of 1990, a man burglarized an upstate New York medical centre morgue and left a note that added insult to injury.

After he had broken into the place, Dennis Crane decided that he didn't approve of the manner in which the cadavers were being sewn up by the medical pathologists. In fact, he declared, he could do a much better job himself.

A police spokesperson said that Crane wrote what amounted to an application for employment. He gave his name, address, and telephone number, and concluded the note with the statement that he was open for a job.

Shrugging aside the technical criticisms of the skills of the resident medical pathologists, security officials used the information that Crane had provided on the note to contact him. When he returned to the morgue on Saturday night, however, he soon learned that he had not been summoned to be interviewed for a job, but to be arrested for burglary.

CHAPTER THREE

CANNIBALISM

SATANIC CANNIBALS TERRORIZE OUR STATE AND NATIONAL PARKS

Throughout the United States, in forested regions, alongside river banks, and on beaches, the mutilated bodies of hitchhikers and transients are being found, their hearts and lungs removed, strips of flesh sliced from their bodies. With each gory new discovery it is becoming startlingly clear that cannibalistic devil-worshipping rites are being conducted in our national and state parks.

In June of 1970, the body of a young schoolteacher was found in a shallow, leaf-covered grave at a roadside park off Highway 74 midway between San Juan Capistrano and Elsinore, California. Her right arm had been severed at the shoulder, and her heart and lungs had been removed from her body. In addition, three of her ribs had been taken and a large strip of flesh had been sliced from her upper right thigh.

When the twenty-year-old monster who had perpetrated such a grisly deed was at last apprehended, he freely admitted that the body parts had been removed from the woman for cannibalistic rites and for sacrifice to Satan.

In July of 1970, a young social worker decided to take a chance on two men who were hitchhiking at the side of the road just outside of Yellowstone Park. Tragically, the act of kindness cost this Good Samaritan his life, for that night, while he slept in a makeshift camp, one of the men killed him, cut out his heart, and ate it.

A few days later, law enforcement officers were summoned to the campsite by a fisherman's discovery of a bloodstained survival knife near a river bank. To their horror and disgust, the officers found what appeared to be human bone fragments, pieces of flesh, teeth, and an ear.

When California police interviewed a vagrant whose suspicious actions had prompted them to detain him, the man confessed that he was troubled by a unique problem. 'I like the taste of human flesh,' he said. 'I am a witch – and I eat people.'

Further interrogation revealed that the cannibalistic vagrant believed himself to be Jesus and thereby felt himself entitled to dine on an occasional man or woman.

The detective sergeant who took down the murderer's statement said that of his many years in police work, this was the weirdest case that he had ever heard of. 'It makes me sick!' he stated with emphasis.

Continued investigation into the background of the self-professed witch, messiah, and cannibal found those who knew him in his home-town in Wyoming to be shocked by the charges levelled against 'such a nice boy'. But a college coed testified how 'really scary' he appeared at a party that she attended, and she swore that she had seen him drink a mug of blood at a beer and pot party in the Tongue River Canyon.

A California beachside park in 1976 produced a number of corpses who had been bludgeoned to death with a heavy metal hammer that left an impression of a pentacle, or five-pointed star, imprinted on their skulls. Bits of flesh had been removed from the victims for supposed cannibalistic purposes.

In Washington State in 1984, several bodies were found in a state park with five-pointed stars and occult symbols carved into the flesh of the victims' chests. Once again, body parts had been carved from the hapless men and women who had come to a park for recreation and who ended being butchered for satanic rituals.

Not long ago, a teenaged boy related accounts of devil-worshipping rites that had taken place in the Big Horn Mountains. Small wild animals had been dedicated to Satan and eaten alive. The informant went on to swear that human blood had been drunk.

HE PROVIDED HIS NEIGHBOURS WITH VENISON BUT HE NEVER SHOT A DEER IN HIS LIFE

In 1957, Ed Gein, an unwed middle-aged farmer from Plainfield, Wisconsin, confessed to stealing a dozen female bodies from fresh graves in the community cemetery. Although he returned most of the pieces after he had dismembered the bodies, he kept a collection of sex parts and noses in a box.

Gein was disposed to nibble at some of the choicest bits and pieces that he carved from the dead, and he also saved ten of the skulls as his special companions. Not one to waste anything, Gein upholstered some of his furniture with human skin.

Gein progressed from grave-robbing to murdering at least two local women. When the sheriff entered the farmhouse, he was horrified to find one of the victims strung up by her heels, decapitated, and eviscerated.

The necrophagiac's neighbours later recalled with great unpleasantness and queasiness of stomach that Gein was forever bringing them portions of 'venison'. While under psychiatric examination, Gein told the analyst that he had never shot a deer in his life.

CHAPTER FOUR

DISORDERLY CONDUCT

SHE WENT TO JAIL FOR SINGING OFF KEY IN THE CHURCH CHOIR

Juanita Almada took the scriptures to heart when they admonished all worshippers to make a joyful noise in the house of God. The trouble was, Juanita sang so loud and so off key that she ended up in jail for singing her praises to the Lord.

The choir singer first got into trouble in June of 1990 when she began to sing a bit louder than the rest of the congregation at Our Lady of Perpetual Help Catholic church in Tulsa, Oklahoma, and she gradually edged about ten feet away from her fellow choir members so she could be closer to the altar at Sunday masses.

Father Robert Watson found Juanita's zealous singing and her proximity to the altar to be 'distracting', and he was dismayed when, over the next several Sundays, she repeated her high-volume singing and her steady approach to the altar. Father Watson tried his best to explain to Juanita that it was important that she stand with the other choir members and that she respect the sanctity of the altar area.

Juanita was troubled and confused by her priest's complaint. She answered him by stating that she sang only to praise God and she did so in the manner in which He told her to sing. She certainly did not wish to disturb Father Watson, but she also very much wished to continue to praise God in the manner He requested.

At the request of Father Watson, a number of parishioners approached Juanita and attempted to reason with the uninhibited choir singer. They tried to make it very clear that no one wished to keep her out of church. All they wanted her to do was to conform to the order of service and to fit in with the rest of the choir members.

The pleas of the priest and his parishioners did nothing to blunt Juanita's enthusiasm for praising God in song. Regretfully, the priest and other members of the congregation deemed her earnest renditions of the hymns to be off key and out of harmony with everyone else.

At last Father Watson reached the limit of his patience, and he obtained a court injunction ordering Juanita Almada to stop singing or worshipping near the altar. When she arrived at Our Lady of Perpetual Help on a Sunday in November to attend mass, she was confronted by the priest.

In response to his demand, Juanita told him that she intended to sing as God directed her. Two policemen had been hiding in trees behind the church, and they approached her and informed her that she was under arrest.

'I didn't know you could be arrested in America for singing the glory of God,' a shocked Juanita exclaimed.

Later, she told reporters how she had been handcuffed 'for what seemed like a lifetime', fingerprinted, forced to pose for mug shots, and kept in a cell for thirteen hours with hardened prostitutes, robbers – and even a murderer. She was charged with disrupting a meeting, a misdemeanour.

Catholic church officials paid Juanita's $400.00 bail, and Father Watson told the court that he would drop all charges against her if she promised not to sing in Our Lady of Perpetual Help church again.

Understandably miffed over the harsh criticism of her heartfelt musical expression of her love for God, Juanita announced that the publicity over her plight had brought her an invitation to sing in the choir of a large Catholic church near by.

'That's where I'll start going,' she said, as though feeling vindicated for her alleged sins of singing off key.

'I won't go back to Father Watson's church,' she added. 'My kids need me too much to be put in jail again.'

THE BIG 220 lb BABY WHO CRASHED DAY-CARE CENTRES

The employees at the Loving Care Children's Centre in Billings, Montana, thought for a terrible moment that their worst nightmare had just walked in the door.

A big baby, standing six-foot-three, weighing 220 lbs, and wearing a diaper, rubber pants, pink dress, and a bonnet stood before them asking directions to the playpen. The behemoth-like 'Baby Huey' also carried a diaper bag, a blanket, and a supply of baby food. Between his smiling lips he sucked on a pacifier that squeaked.

Nervous laughter issued from the staff. The weirdo standing before them had called earlier and claimed to be a college student who was forced to atone for cheating on a test by acting like a baby.

But now that he was here, the day-care staffers were reluctant to allow him to waddle in among their infant charges. After all, why should they participate in such bizarre punishment from the college? And what rational and responsible professor would send a student dressed in such a manner to disturb the children at a day-care centre?

When the brute in the pink dress and bonnet asked to lie down among the tiny tots at naptime, they became increasingly suspicious and ill at ease. Refusing to allow him to lie among the children, they placed him in a separate room where he snuggled under his baby blanket.

The monstrous infant's plans for additional playpen fun were quickly circumvented when a supervisor recognized him as Andy Bolton, a twenty-two-year-old peculiar person who got his kicks from dressing up in baby clothes and attempting to crash day-care centres. The supervisor recalled a prior incident when Bolton had attempted to invade another day-care centre.

Police were summoned to take the big baby into custody. The City Prosecutor stated that Bolton had donned his pink bonnet and diapers a number of times at other day-care centres in the city.

Bolton later pleaded no contest to a charge of lewd behaviour. He was advised to secure counselling, and the judge told him that if he didn't seek to crash any more day-care centres for a year, she would dismiss the charges.

IT COST THE LADY TOURIST A HEFTY FINE TO FIND OUT WHAT A SCOTSMAN WEARS UNDER HIS KILT!

Jo Carlin, a forty-eight-year-old tourist from Syracuse, New York, could not resist discovering for herself the answer to the age-old query, 'What does a Scotsman wear under his kilt?'

She managed to get her peek but she was sentenced to spend one night in an Edinburgh jail and fined £156.

Jo, a retired schoolteacher, was vacationing in Scotland with her friend Amy in the spring of 1988. When the two ladies stood before historic Edinburgh Castle and saw all the handsome guardsmen in their kilts, Jo's curiosity got the better of her.

She strolled casually over to a guardsman who stood on duty in front of his sentry box, then she purposely dropped a coin on to the pavement. As she bent down to recover her coin, she lifted up the Scotsman's kilt and took a peek.

'That's when all blazes broke loose!' Jo recalled. The guardsman, who acted totally nonplussed and shocked, grabbed her by the arm. A sergeant arrived and called the police. In an astonishingly rapid blur of minutes, she stood before a judge, charged with malicious mischief.

The Scots are not without their sense of humour, for even the judge had to stifle his laughter when he learned the nature of the charges against Jo Carlin. But he rapped his gavel, called for order, and admonished her that a lively curiosity should never overpower the urge to commit a wanton invasion of another's privacy.

Later, Jo admitted that she was sorry that she had perpetrated such an expensive prank. The amount of the fine and the night in jail surprised the 'heck' out of her.

Back in Syracuse, she has the same answer for everyone who asks her, well, just what does a Scotsman wear under his kilt? 'Go have a look for yourself!'

TAUGHT THE ABCS IN PRISON, CON WRITES DEATH THREATS TO JUDGES

When Albert Downe was sentenced to ten years in a Canadian penitentiary for arson, he was totally illiterate, unable to read or write. As an integral part of Downe's rehabilitation programme, the correctional authorities deemed it appropriate to teach him reading and writing skills.

Once he had mastered his new-found abilities with the *ABC*s, Downe took pen in hand and began writing threatening letters to four district court judges. Since men and women in such positions are not amused by death threats and tend to take them quite seriously, Downe, in the summer of 1989, was taken to court and given an additional four years in prison for his unappreciated pen pal endeavours.

Downe's plea was that he had hoped the death threats would convince prison authorities that he belonged in a pyschiatric hospital for the criminally insane, rather than a penitentiary. He claimed that he had been trying to be placed in a treatment programme for arsonists since his arrival in the penitentiary.

Downe's defence attorney remarked on the irony of the whole affair. After all, he mused, it was the correctional authorities who took it upon themselves to teach Downe to read and to write. If Albert Downe had remained illiterate, he wouldn't have been able to write the death threats to the judges and he would have stayed out of trouble.

A little knowledge, improperly channelled, can be a dangerous thing.

FURIOUS FARMER BLASTS TOWN HALL WITH SIX TONS OF MANURE

For forty-five years, sixty-three-year-old former boxer David Cannon worked a farm outside of Morpeth, England. For years he'd had his eye on a piece of land near his property where he yearned to build a retirement home for himself and his wife.

In 1985, he filed an application for a building permit to construct his dream home but his request was denied. Town planners said that the building of any home in that area was prohibited.

Cannon, perturbed, pointed out that a house had stood on that land for generations.

Officials at the Town Hall replied that the house had been demolished several years ago and, since then, new laws prohibited any building in the area.

Desiring to follow the letter of the law, Cannon filed a

second application... then a third... and, in the summer of 1992, a fourth. Each one of his requests was denied.

'This is really "B S",' the farmer stormed. 'The Town Hall has been giving it to me for seven years, so it is time that they got some of it back!'

Cannon, who, in addition to raising crops, managed to keep a prize-winning herd of cattle, loaded six tons of manure into his muck spreader, pulled it alongside of the Town Hall in Morpeth, and let fly.

Eight times he drove up and down beside the building until he had blasted his entire load at the Town Hall. Stunned employees ran for cover as the foul-smelling liquid cow dung sprayed through open windows and splattered their desks, chairs, computers, and carpets.

'They were dumping on me,' Cannon told journalist John Cooke, 'so I decided the best protest I could make was to dump on them. They should be honoured. That was my best cow manure from my prize-winning herd.'

Town officials insisted that they had not intended to pick on the feisty farmer. They argued that they had turned down similar applications from hundreds of other people, and they maintained that it would be unfair to accept his just because he had raised a stink.

David Cannon was arrested for disturbing the peace and made to bear the cost of cleaning up the six tons of manure. He remained unrepentant, however. His pungent protest seemed to him to be tit for tat.

CHAPTER FIVE

FRAUD

THE LIVING FLAME THAT SOUGHT TO CONSUME LONDON

It was 1919 and not long since the stalwart British had put behind them the Great War. But while the majority of Londoners thanked God that the white cliffs of Dover still stood firm and time could still be measured by the ticking of Big Ben, a number of their fellow citizens had a new worry: great cosmic forces were about to war in their own beloved city. A handsome spellbinder who called himself 'Osiris Reincarnated' was warning his followers that if they remained in London they would be destroyed by Set, the fierce Egyptian devil-in-chief and his own half-brother, long since disowned by their wise mother Nut.

Osiris Reincarnated (Edvaard Admusson) claimed that he was looking after the welfare and preservation of his cult, the Living Flame, by advising its members to leave the city. At the same time, he was watching his own backside, because the good folk of London were beginning to realize that this was no ordinary Church with which their loved ones were linked, even though there might be landed gentry among the congregation. There was also word that a number of relatives of certain of Osiris' parishioners had suggested that the courts should look into this particular prophet and assess just exactly what it was that he preached.

Edvaard Admusson had grown up in Waukegan, Illinois, the son of a travelling salesman father and an amateur occultist mother. At his mother's knee little Eddie had learned much about the many mystical philosophies, and he also divined that a great many people are inclined to believe strange things. As he matured, he had decided that the myths of the most obscure cults could have a very broad appeal if they were presented with imagination and zeal.

During World War I, Edvaard enlisted in the US Navy to avoid the draft, a move that could not have been better planned had he known the outcome. His duty took him to Alexandria, Egypt, and it was here that he was to master the mythology of the ancient religion of the pharaohs.

He became particularly fascinated by the accounts of Isis and Osiris, for to these ancient gods worshippers had brought gifts, rather than prayers. That was precisely what Edvaard wanted for his future.

The war passed without troubling Edvaard unduly, and he remained in Alexandria studying the old myths with a fervour that surely would have qualified him to earn a doctorate in Egyptian studies.

Soon after the Armistice was signed on 11 November 1918, Edvaard made the decision to travel to London to ply his new-found trade, godhood. He was aware that at that time London was quite likely the world centre of cultist activity – and over and above that, the city was suffering a terrible man shortage due to the casualties of the war. In addition to a passion for the ancient Egyptian gods, Edvaard had developed an insatiable fancy for the ladies, and they were to be the primary targets of the cult of the Living Flame.

The god-being who walked among humans remained inactive for a time until he happened to hear mention of the Lord and Lady Blaykelocke, a titled couple who, it seemed, had an affinity for cultic mysticism. When Edvaard learned further that Lady Blaykelocke was bedridden with a chronic illness, he saw a way to ingratiate himself into the family confidence – and the family fortune.

Edvaard identified himself to Lord Eustace Blaykelocke

as Osiris Reincarnated and claimed that he could heal his wife, Lady Sabrina. Upon admittance to the lady's bedchambers, he intuitively diagnosed her illness to be psychosomatic. With the end of the war, Lady Sabrina was suffering only from an affliction known as boredom for over the past several years, both she and her husband had been extremely active in the defence effort.

The presence of Osiris Reincarnated was just what Lady Sabrina needed to embark upon a process of rejuvenation. Without hesitation, she permitted a physical examination and Edvaard, drawing upon his libidinous hoard of talents, gave her the massage of her life.

With the rebirth of Lady Sabrina, there also blossomed the birth of the cult of the Living Flame. Osiris Reincarnated incorporated the lord and lady – and a substantial amount of their money – into the Living Flame, then developed the credo by which its members should guide their lives.

'Religion,' Osiris cheerfully stated, 'is easy to understand. Be good. That is all there is to it. In sex, never be vulgar, just efficient. In true love between humans, there can be no friction and no jealousies. The first thing to learn is that love is the key to the divine rationalization of sex. Between lovers, the sexual relationship is the highest expression of love. There is no place for prudery in passions that spring from love. Society has erred blindly in its suppression of sex by mock morality. Suppression is the most powerful stimulant for the arousing of the vulgar instincts.'

Free, uninhibited sex! The concept was very appealing in post-war London. Osiris, too, had more than a nibbler's appetite for the pleasures of the flesh, and he was constantly seen in the company of one of his more attractive disciples.

In spirit, at least, Osiris gave as much as he received. He took a direct personal interest in his clients, encouraged them to develop themselves as women, as well as love objects, and kept the cult small enough so that he never lost track of each individual's progress.

One of his more devoted followers was Phyllis Ramsford, who, although not a beautiful girl, was vivacious and possessed of a magnificent body that had attracted Edvaard's roving eye. Phyllis had been drawn to one of the early meetings at the Blaykelocke mansion, and whatever her motivation had been in attending a meeting of the cult, she saw what she wanted in Edvaard. Osiris encouraged Phyllis to realize her secret desire to be a dancer and soon she headed up the Virgin Corps, the naked chorus line that the Master used frequently in his ceremonies.

Throughout her association with the cult, Phyllis remained Edvaard's favourite, though not his exclusively. In the cult no one had sole rights to any other member. It was share, sample, and cohabit as one chose.

The meetings of the Living Flame were not that difficult to attend, and should an irate relative have managed to slip in to check on one of the family, the 'church service' might well have presented him with the shock of his life.

The scene before him would have appeared much like a pageant depicting a tableau of antiquity – except that few of the actors and actresses wore any clothing. The principal patrons, Lord Eustace and Lady Sabrina, occupied a place of honour in the setting. Nude dancers gyrated through a preliminary ritual, and then Osiris himself would come forward to address the assembled disciples.

Clad only in tight-fitting breeches and a cloak decorated with mystical symbols, Osiris, his body glistening from perfumed olive oil and his very presence emitting an aura of sensuality, raised his hands and reminded his devout followers: 'The power of love has no equal. Be not inhibited, for in love lies the salvation of us all.'

Osiris would next begin a series of chants, and there would be more dancing, with everyone taking part. As the fervour of the party grew, the music would increase in tempo, and the incantations would become more delirious – until it appeared that everyone in the manor was under the mesmerizing spell of Eros. Those who still wore clothing would tear the restricting garments from their bodies. Those already naked would exhibit the power of love and turn up their private 'living flames'. Women would roll about on the floor, as though trying to cast off demons, then reach for the decorative phallic symbols set into the walls. One by one, Osiris, Lord Eustace, and the other male members of the cult would choose their bride of the night and disappear into one of the adjoining rooms.

And so the 'church service' would go, and such was the substance of the Living Flame – in spite of the growing numbers of Londoners who were beginning to clamour to have the cult dispersed.

Osiris, however, was one jump ahead of his detractors. Before they could put any substance into their feelings, he had informed his faithful that he would lead a series of advance parties to the island of San Marcos, located in the gulf of Lower California off the coast of Mexico, and thus pave the way for the rest of them to join them. His loyal followers readily accepted his revelation from Mother Nut and were as eager to leave London as he. Osiris had been their guiding light and had performed miracles for them far outside the realm of any earthly healer.

The downfall of the Living Flame occurred in 1920 when General Obregon became President of Mexico and let it be known that the cultist known as Osiris Reincarnated would be arrested if he returned to San Marcos with another of his 'advance parties'. It was not so much that the licentious activities of the cult offended General Obregon – but the vast amounts of Mexican gold that Edvaard had been smuggling out of the country had upset him terribly.

'I must go to seek a new place for us,' Osiris told Lady Sabrina on the eve of his departure. 'You are the only one I shall tell for fear of disturbing the tranquillity of the rest.'

The lady said that she understood his mission, and she sent him on his way with a considerable sum of money from the treasury of the Living Flame. Unbeknownst to the loyal lady, Edvaard also took along his own personal fortune.

No more was ever heard of Osiris Reincarnated. Some investigators say that he bought a yacht in New York with the money from the treasury of the Living Flame and manned it with a beautiful chorus girl as co-captain and a lusty crew of converts to 'Noah's Ark of Love', his latest cult. Others say that Edvaard Admusson died in Switzerland after living an exceedingly full life.

'GOAT GLANDS' BRINKLEY – THE GREAT REJUVENATOR WHO FOUND THE FOUNTAIN OF YOUTH

In the 1920s, John Romulus Brinkley sold the entire Midwest on the notion that he had personal control of the fountain of youth. He had convinced worn and ageing males that he could put new 'oomph' in their love life. The secret Brinkley proclaimed daily from his own powerful radio station, KFKB, was in the glands.

'A man is no older than his glands,' were the words that vibrated over the airwaves for over fifteen hours a day, and Dr John R. Brinkley offered to make a man's glands as young as... well, at least as young as the goats he castrated.

For several years, Brinkley had sensed that Americans of every class would clamour to let him take their money if he could somehow convince them that eternal youth would be theirs in return. His earlier schemes had been, perhaps, a bit too scientific in tone to capture the imagination of the ordinary mind, but when he hit on the fantasy of substituting the glands of the proverbial, everlastingly virile goat for those of a tired old man, his practice began to thrive.

When 'Goat Glands' Brinkley completed his con, all the run-of-the-mill quacks had been put to shame. Dr Brinkley transformed his magical, fairy-tale pitch into a ten-million-dollar empire.

Born in Beta, South Carolina, in 1885, Brinkley's mother died before he reached the age of six, and his father passed away by the time he was ten. Left in the poverty-stricken home of an aunt, he sought escape; when he reached the age of sixteen, he jumped at the chance.

Young John dreamed of a life much better than the one that fate had provided for him in the Carolina hills, and his travels took him to Baltimore, where he applied for admission to the Johns Hopkins University Medical School. His application was reviewed and refused, and the dejected youth might have returned to Beta empty handed if it had not been for a smooth-talking fellow who approached him with a story about a 'private' medical school that taught folks how to be doctors by correspondence. All Brinkley had to do was to sign on the dotted line.

Eager to make his mark in the medical world, John Romulus Brinkley jumped at the opportunity. The course covered only herbal medicine, but this made no difference to the enthusiastic young man. It was not until four years later that several doctors emphatically informed him that 'roots and bay leaves' were on the way out.

Disgusted, Brinkley headed back for Beta, where he married Sally Wilke and tried to make a life in his hometown. But after he had seen the much larger cities of the eastern seaboard, Beta's one-horse pace seemed intolerable. John and Sally packed their bags and headed for Chicago.

With his excellent background in herbal medicine, Brinkley enrolled in an advanced course at Bennett Medical College. He continued his studies, and after a few years of diligent application, he was awarded a diploma from the Eclectic Medical University of Kansas City. With this formidable-sounding institution behind him, he became Dr J. R. Brinkley, and he and Sally travelled east to New York, where he flim-flammed the city out of a permit to set up a shop as a dealer in herbs.

But things were just as the orthodox medical doctors had advised him: roots weren't selling.

Once again, Brinkley was on the edge of despair when a fellow herbalist told him that he knew how to bring in all the money that they would ever need. Brinkley gave the man his undivided attention, and the newly formed medical team set up shop in Greenville, South Carolina, as 'electro-medical specialists'.

Disgusted with her husband's shady schemes, Sally asked Brinkley for a divorce, and when he would not give her one, she walked out on him, taking their child with her. Brinkley went after her and brought her back two times before he finally realized that any personal magnetism he might have had that had once attracted Sally had long since fizzled. At last he gave up and granted her the divorce.

Forever restless, Brinkley left his partner and the electro-medical speciality and travelled through Tennessee and Arkansas, picking up practitioner's licences in both states. His next lengthy stop would be in Kansas.

He arrived in the small town of Fulton with a new wife and a head buzzing with money-making ideas. After only six months' residence, the townspeople elected him mayor, and Brinkley began to groom a goatee that he hoped would help him to convince more people that he was a genuine medical doctor than the parchment from the Eclectic Medical University seemed to be able to do.

On 7 October 1917, Brinkley heard the drumbeat of his destiny and moved to Milford, Kansas. The town had neither a doctor nor a hospital, and it looked like easy pickings. Brinkley opened a drugstore and once again established a medical practice on the strength of his questionable diploma.

It was about this time that he began reading about the research of a Russian scientist working in Paris who was trying to rejuvenate chimpanzees by switching their glands around. Serge Voronoff was actually a serious scientist, performing experimental graftings on his laboratory animals in the interest of science and humanity. Scientifically, Voronoff's results were inconclusive, but when Brinkley's fertile imagination began to fantasize about the experiments, he could see dollar signs rolling up before his eyes.

Goats, he mused, would be more accessible to him in Kansas. And besides, goats were considered to be hornier, lustier, and more virile than any monkeys he had ever heard of. All it would take, he speculated as the con took shape in his mind, would be a few affidavits from satisfied customers *and their wives* to give him a line of customers clamouring for goat-gland transplants and super sex lives.

By August of 1918 his business had expanded so much that he had a fifty-bed hospital constructed to handle the steady flow of patients through Milford. The hospital was not second rate in any department. Brinkley's assistants were well dressed; the rooms were as sterile as those in any other hospital; and the facilities were up-to-the-minute.

It is strange to note that very few of Dr Brinkley's patients ever complained that the operation was unsuccessful. Most of them left Milford feeling potent again – and after they reached home, reports from their wives confirmed the astounding fact. It would seem that very little was known about the power of suggestion in the Roaring Twenties.

With the gland business booming, Brinkley faced a serious shortage of healthy Kansas goats. He used the money gained (fifty patients a week at $750 a patient) to build a spur line into Milford from a nearby railway. The goats began arriving from Arkansas and Tennessee by the carload.

Although the money kept pouring in, Brinkley, ever alert for a new source of income, was advised by a Kansas City advertising man to go into radio. It sounded like a very good way to sell himself and his operations, so Brinkley erected KFKB (Kansas First, Kansas Best) and began broadcasting across the nation's midsection for over fifteen hours a day. He not only sold goat-gland transplants, but he dug back into his past of herb peddling to sell all sorts of cures over the air. The kickbacks that he began receiving from druggists all over the country soon equalled his income from the goat-gland business.

As he reached the apex of his career, Brinkley began to hear annoying voices of dissent from around the nation. At first, he could not hear them above the roar of the money cascading around him, but later he came to understand that some of the complainants had more clout than he had estimated.

The American Medical Association began to howl about the fact that Dr Brinkley had a rather shoddy education and had, in effect, bought his diploma. It was strongly argued that Brinkley should be brought to trial and be made to answer the charges brought by his so-called medical peers. But Kansas loved John Brinkley, and they refused to ship him off somewhere back East for an inquisition.

But the wall Dr Brinkley had built around himself had begun to crack. In 1930, a reporter from the Kansas City *Star* began banging out articles that accused Dr John 'Goat Glands' Brinkley of everything from mutilation to murder. The *Star* had dug up evidence that Brinkley's operations were not permanently successful and that at least one man, a New Jersey carpenter, had died of tetanus after taking the Brinkley treatment.

Brinkley found himself fighting a losing battle. When officials in Kansas were confronted with the death certificates of forty-two patients who had died under Brinkley's care, they had no choice but to revoke his licence.

Brinkley circumvented that crisis by hiring regularly licensed surgeons to perform the operations for him, but he was in a battle to save his money-making radio station as well.

In Washington, DC, Brinkley took the stand as a sort of character witness for himself and explained how he had given new life to seven newspapermen from Los Angeles.

But the Kansas City *Star* reporter who had begun the deadly avalanche of accusations jumped up and shouted, 'Yes, except that one died!'

The charge was devastating. Although Brinkley won the right to broadcast while he was making an appeal to higher courts, he could not forestall the inevitable.

Perhaps hoping to gain enough power in Kansas to control the boards and legislators, Brinkley announced his candidacy for governor. Since he had announced too late to be placed on the ballot, Brinkley ran as a write-in candidate and was barely nosed out by his opponents. Although he had retained a general, statewide popularity, there was no question that he had begun an inexorable slide downward.

Brinkley sold the Kansas radio station and set off to build one south of the border that would thunderously blast his message from Mexico into the South and the Southwest.

Convinced that the people of Kansas still loved him, Brinkley ran once again for governor in 1932, but he was nosed out by Alf Landon.

Out of national embarrassment, the State Department began putting pressure on the Mexican government to shut down Brinkley's border blaster. By this time, Brinkley was desperately clinging to a threatened ten-million-dollar empire, and he acquiesced to the wishes of the Mexican authorities only when troops showed up at the station's studios.

After Brinkley's powerful, influential radio voice had been silenced, medical authorities began levelling their heavy guns at him from all sides. Brinkley tried to sue for libel, but the courts were quick to rule against him.

By 1941, the Great Rejuvenator had so many lawsuits against him that a court in Texas declared him to be bankrupt.

In May of 1942, at the age of fifty-six, John Romulus Brinkley died.

THE WAYWARD PRIEST WANTED TO CASH IN ON JUDGEMENT DAY

There was an expression of urgency on the face of Father Hans Mueller on that dreary February day in 1950 as he stepped up to address the emergency meeting of his parish.

'Sister Greta has received a vision from heaven,' he told the assembled congregation. 'The message says that in 1953 there will be a series of cataclysms that will destroy the world as we know it. We will be told a safe place to gather in order to be spared the destruction that will visit the rest of the Earth.'

Father Mueller's announcement bit sharply into the hearts of his devout parishioners, but they rose boldly to meet the challenge. After all, if Sister Greta had said so, it must be true. Was she not the one who was able to communicate directly with Christ?

Father Mueller had first met Sister Greta at a religious conference. At the time, the Catholic nun had been credited with having received several visions in which she had been given sage advice by the Holy Mother.

Father Mueller, who harboured more than a bit of larceny in his heart, saw in the good sister a latent talent that might one day be put to use for his own benefit. He persuaded his superiors to permit Sister Greta to visit his area, the town of Bremen, Germany, and he personally saw to her lodging in the fine house of his secret mistress, Margaret Kuhlmann.

The unscrupulous priest immediately allowed word to seep to his parishioners that Sister Greta had been blessed with the gift of extraordinary communicative powers with the divine, thus laying the basic groundwork for the confidence job that he was about to pull on them. When the townsfolk had been sufficiently primed, he called them to an emergency session of the congregation and revealed the startling orders from on high: a secret retreat must be built.

Under the guidance of Father Mueller, the New Jerusalem Society was formed, and the devout believers began pouring in contributions. The crafty priest, as the creator and the head of the Society, was to undertake the actual building of the secret hideaway. For such an endeavour, he preached incessantly, much money would be needed.

Since the Roman Catholic Church has always maintained a fairly good line of communication from parish to hierarchy, it was not terribly long before his superiors got wind of the questionable New Jerusalem Society, and they sent representatives to investigate the bizarre reports from Bremen. When they learned that Father Mueller was not only living with a mistress but that she had borne him two children, they immediately brought punitive action upon the errant clergyman. Such conduct, the Church superiors declared, could not be tolerated. Father Mueller was defrocked and given his orders of expulsion.

The publishing of such ecclesiastical edicts against the priest was not enough to sway the local citizenry of Bremen from their firm belief that the end of the world was at hand. They continued to contribute to the building of the retreat, and Mueller continued to collect their money. To add to the mystery, he informed them that the hideaway was being built in the strictest secrecy and that only he knew its exact location.

Although a year passed without any indication of great catastrophes, Mueller realized that he had far too good a con going to allow a little matter like a dearth of disasters to stop him from continuing to harvest the congregation of Bremen. He merely prolonged things by revealing that Sister Greta had been in contact with heaven once again and had received the divine pronouncement that the end of the world had been postponed until 1955.

'It was a decision of mercy,' he assured them. 'For we have not yet had enough money to be able to stock the retreat with food and medical supplies. We must have more money before Judgement Day is upon us.'

And more money came. Some of the more devout sold everything they had and turned all the money over to Mueller for a guaranteed cottage in the secret retreat.

As might be expected, there were a few townspeople who did not believe in Mueller's self-appointed role as the twentieth-century Jeremiah. Investigations disclosed the discomforting fact that the defrocked priest had been spending the money on luxuries, furnishing the house in which he lived with Margaret Kuhlmann, and buying a new Porsche. It was also learned that the remainder of the money collected from the parishioners had been deposited in Mueller's personal bank account. Further, it was discovered that the prophet Sister Greta was being held in the Mueller house against her will.

It was that final ugly bit of intelligence that at last swayed Mueller's true believers. At the first opportunity, they rescued Sister Greta and delivered her to a convent near Munich.

When they were certain that her welfare was assured, they obtained the aid of a Catholic priest and undertook legal action against Mueller and Margaret Kuhlmann: but when the German police arrived to arrest the two, they found them gone. The Porsche and the balance of Mueller's bank account had also disappeared.

Nothing more was heard of the perverse mayor of New Jerusalem until eight years later in 1963, when Mueller was arrested and charged with the torture and murder of a teenaged girl.

It seems that while hiding from the police, Mueller had founded a flagellant cult, the Disciplined Society for Love. In his new organization, Mueller's interests had changed from monetary manipulations to a kind of barbaric sadism. And it was this twisted mode of sexual release that brought about the death of Karol Hinrichsen.

The unfortunate girl had been the daughter of an old crony

of Mueller's, Emil Hinrichsen, the man he had formerly installed as an officer of the New Jerusalem Society. The prudish Hinrichsen had often feared that his daughter was obsessed with lustfulness and worldliness, traits commonly diagnosed as symptoms of demonic possession. So he had taken Karol along with him to one of the Society for Love meetings in March of 1963. It was the cult's sworn duty to drive all trace of influencing demons from sinful bodies – especially the sinful bodies of nubile young women.

Methodically, as was directed by the rites of their ceremonies, Mueller, with the faithful Margaret Kuhlmann at his side, ordered an initial flogging of the girl in an effort to drive evil from her. After the perfunctory lashing, the methods of demon control became hideously and painfully inventive.

The lengthy and bloody exorcism conducted by Mueller proved to be inconclusive. Whether or not any demons were driven from her body, the teenager's life spark could not withstand the terrible punishment of the ritual torture. Karol Hinrichsen would never entertain another licentious thought. The next morning her family found her dead in her bed.

A comprehensive investigation followed, and all who were connected with the sex cult's torture of the girl were brought to trial, including Father Mueller and Margaret Kuhlmann. But the termination of the perverse activities of the defrocked priest could be of little recompense to the murdered girl.

WANTED: A WOMAN TO BEAR THE CHILD OF GOD – INTERESTED PARTIES REPLY TO JESUS AND THE MOTHER SPIRIT

With great stress and difficulty, Daisy Pollex Adams slowly unravelled her testimony in front of the English court.

'I was sent to London by my parents to live with those two!' she said, casting a contemptuous glance at the co-defendants. 'They were supposed to see to my proper religious and worldly education. Instead, they are the most evil people I have ever known!'

The defendants remained composed in their seats, occasionally firing a question in self-examination. They were confident that they could defeat the case against them. After all, they were the present physical embodiments of Jesus Christ and the Holy Mother Spirit.

On a more earthly level, they were Frank Dutton Jackson and Editha Loleta Jackson, husband and wife, also known as Theo Horos and the Swami. The Swami had grown to be a fat, grotesque, beastly looking thing, who usually adorned herself in white satin robes of Grecian design. Her husband was very thin and spindly and not nearly as flamboyant in his dress. A greater physical contrast in man and wife would hardly be possible. Morally, however, they were as similar as cartridges in the chambers of a revolver.

At the turn of the century, Theo and the Swami achieved notoriety throughout most of the civilized world and were pursued by as many law-enforcement agencies as countries they had visited. Their escapades carried them across three continents, and their victims numbered into the thousands.

The name of their game was confidence; their particular suit was religion. They were cultists, and as money was not enough to satisfy their greed, they were also inclined to practice whatever sexual perversions struck their fancy. Their acts of carnal perversions came to light during their hearing in October of 1901 and were instrumental in sending them away for long sentences of penal servitude.

Originally, on 26 September, they had been brought before the magistrate at Marylebone police court on charges of cheating and defrauding one Vera Croysdale of several articles of jewellery. Miss Croysdale had been bamboozled into joining their religious order and had fallen completely under the domination of Theo and the Swami, who was, at that time, posing as her husband's mother.

Vera had become a true believer, and she had freely given herself sexually to Theo without question, without restraint. Theo's time-tested seduction gambit was to convince the female that since he was Jesus Christ, the Son of God, returned to earth, she may, if sperm, egg, and Holy Spirit connected, become the new mother of God.

Whether or not Vera Croysdale had any actual designs on becoming the Mother of God was never determined, but it was apparent from the loving letters that she wrote to Theo that she enjoyed a comfortable and enjoyable relationship with the odd couple. The infringement of her honour was not her charge. It was when she had mysteriously 'lost' her jewellery and other items of value and later saw the same pieces in the window of a pawnshop that she decided that the work of God had taken on a decidedly more earthbound nature.

Vera confronted Theo with her evidence, but he tried to brush her accusations aside, saying, 'Those were gifts laid on the altar of God!'

No longer blinded by promises of becoming the Mother of God, Vera Croysdale went to the police and made a formal complaint. The Swami and Theo were unsuccessful in their attempt to leave the city one step ahead of the authorities, and on 26 September 1901, they were brought before Magistrate Curtis Bennett to answer the charges brought by Miss Croysdale.

During the ensuing investigation, more of the unholy pair's victims dropped their mantles of pride and embarrassment and came forward with tales of woe. Perhaps the most repulsive was the account of Daisy Adams, a girl of sixteen, who stated that Theo had not only raped her but had done so under the most revolting of circumstances.

Miss Adams told the court of her journey to London with the Swami and Theo and described her initiation into the sacred mysteries of their cult of Theocratic Unity. Theo had explained to her the obligations of the religion, then revealed that he was the Son of God. Daisy was told that the Mother Spirit had visited him and declared that she was to be his wife and to bear the new Son of God.

'I asked him if the Mother Spirit would visit me, too,' Daisy told the court. 'Theo replied that she would when I had given up the world and had got to the life which he would teach me. But he said that I must be obedient to all of his orders and do everything that he told me. He was so convincing and sincere that I just couldn't help myself. I thought that he truly was very close to being something like Christ.'

Daisy testified that Theo had taken her to bed with him and had instructed her that by giving him her body she would bring forth the Motherhood of God. But to her horror, the dishevelled hulk of the Swami arrived to observe the planting of the holy seed.

'I just knew that that couldn't be the bed of Christ,' Daisy stated. 'I wanted to get up and leave, but she grabbed me and stopped me. She told me how much Theo really loved me and how, next to the Spirit Mother, I was really dear to his heart.

'But I didn't believe them any more, and I wanted to get out of there. I struggled, but she pinned my arms and held me down. Honestly, I couldn't move!'

There was a slight murmur as the court studied the Swami and appraised the restraining bulk of her excessive flesh.

The girl flushed, but found enough composure to continue. 'That was when... while she was holding me down... that he... that he did *it*.' Daisy said the words very quickly, as though she were ashamed that she could think of no other more suitable terminology for the sex act.

Theo and the Swami were brought to trial on the rape charge, the most serious of the indictments.

In an attempt to conduct their own defence, the Swami did their case more harm than good. By making sarcastic interjections and by rambling on with sentences so long that often her thoughts were either lost or confused, she seemed to be attempting to make a mockery of the trial, the witnesses, the court officials, and the gallery of spectators. She and Theo were so inept in their closing remarks that it took the jury only five minutes to return a guilty decree against both of them.

BY DISPLAYING HER WEBBED FEET, SHE PROVED SHE WAS NOT THE CORPSE IN THE GRAVE

On a midnight at London Bridge in February of 1900, the body of a woman was found floating in the murky waters. The corpse was taken to a mortuary, and there her expensive clothing was removed.

The woman was young – around twenty years old, it was judged. Her clothing bore old laundry marks, and each of her silken garments bore a coronet and the initials 'F. D.'

The body had been in the water so long that a facial identification was impossible. Many people who had missing female relatives viewed the corpse, but none could identify her.

Eventually, the press photographs were seen by a woman in France, who declared that the unidentified body was that of her daughter, Fleur Duval. Mrs Duval travelled to London and identified the clothing and the dead girl's blonde hair.

Tearfully, she had the remains transported to France and interred in a family plot. The headstone bore the name Fleur Duval.

Months passed and the matter seemed quite forgotten until a woman was arrested in London and charged with some petty offences. She identified herself as a Frenchwoman and gave her name as Fleur Duval. Furthermore, she claimed that she had been employed as a governess and had fallen upon hard times.

A journalist with a long memory visited the young Frenchwoman and informed her that a countrywoman with her exact name had been found floating in the waters near London Bridge. Miss Duval protested that the body that had been found was certainly not her own.

When experienced police officials suggested that Fleur Duval may have arranged the deceased woman's demise in an attempt to establish another identity, she protested her innocence of murder and confessed that she had been serving a prison sentence at the time under another name. A brief investigation established the fact that she was telling the truth.

Miss Duval told the authorities that she had originally come to England because she had had an unhappy home life. She had become a governess for a time, but she had been dismissed.

Suddenly bereft of any means of income, she had sold some of her expensive clothing. Later, even more desperate to survive, she had turned to shoplifting. She had been caught and sentenced to a brief imprisonment.

The journalist accompanied Fleur Duval to France, where they contacted her mother. But Madame Duval insisted that the girl was an impostor.

Fleur, on the other hand, was shocked at her mother's denial of their relationship, but she was able to prove beyond all doubt that she was the daughter of Madame Duval.

When the case came at last to the French courts, it was revealed that Fleur's grandfather, a man of title, had left a large sum of money to her that she could claim on her twenty-first birthday. If Fleur should die before that date, the estate was to go to her mother and brother. Madame Duval took advantage of the unknown female body that had been pulled out of the waters near London Bridge – and since the corpse was conveniently wearing Fleur's clothing, she 'identified' it as that of her daughter.

It was later proved that Madame Duval could not have mistaken the unidentified corpse as Fleur's, for Fleur had webbed feet, like a duck, while the unknown woman had normal feet.

It was never established whose body had been buried in the Duval family plot. Madame Duval had to return the money and the estate to her daughter, but there was no other punishment, as she had employed very clever lawyers.

CHAPTER SIX

HOMICIDE

A STRANGE TALE OF TWO MURDERED IRENES

Irene Munro was a pretty Scottish typist who, in August 1920, went for a summer holiday at Eastbourne, Sussex, not dreaming that she was soon to die.

There was at that time a stretch of comparatively lonely beach at Eastbourne known as the Crumbles, a sinister place that had been the scene of several murders. It was on the sands there on 20 August 1920 that children discovered the body of the luckless Irene Munro. She had been hurriedly buried on the beach, but the tide had exposed one of her feet.

Within a few hours, Chief Inspector Mercer of Scotland Yard arrived on the scene to conduct the official investigation of the case. Medical examination revealed that Irene had been badly and brutally beaten and that her agony had at last been ended by the murderer or murderers dropping a heavy boulder on her head.

A background investigation of the girl's life was ordered, and subsequent research yielded not a single clue whatsoever as to why she should have been murdered. Since she appeared to have had no known enemies or anyone who would wish her dead, Chief Inspector Mercer could only conclude that her death had occurred as the result of meeting with – and being attacked by – person or persons unknown.

Harold Speer, a well-known British journalist of the day,

became intrigued by the case of the unfortunate Irene. He contacted a spiritualist medium with whom he was acquainted named Miss Groebel, who agreed to accompany him to the scene of the crime on the Crumbles at Eastbourne. Speer took with them some of the victim's clothing obtained from her family.

In his book *The Secret History of Great Crimes*, Speer reports that the medium began to pick up psychic impressions as soon as she handled the young woman's clothes. They stood alone at night in the eerie quiet of the Crumbles and, as she began to speak, the familiar voice of Miss Groebel was replaced by a tone entirely different from her usual manner of speaking. The experienced journalist admitted that never before had he experienced such an uncanny scene.

While the voice of the murdered Irene Munro came from the lips of the medium, Speer kept a shorthand record of the words. After she had given a description of the two men who had slain her and a graphic account of her death, the spirit concluded with the words: 'I see my murderers now at a small hotel which has a white front. It is called the Albemarle.'

On the following day, Speer handed his notes to Chief Inspector Mercer, who did not scoff at the information. Rather, he went himself to the Albemarle Hotel and there he encountered two young men named Jack Alfred Field and William Thomas Gray. Both men were later arrested and charged with the murder of Irene Munro.

The details of the crime were exactly as relayed by Irene through the mediumship of Miss Groebel. Field and Gray had met Irene casually, and they had walked together along the Crumbles. The two men decided to steal her handbag and when she resisted, they struck her several times with a walking stick. Miss Munro had fallen and Field and Gray, confused and muddled with panic, crushed her skull with a boulder and buried her body on the beach.

Once the bloody deed was done, Field and Gray made off with the few pounds in the handbag and eventually made their way to the Albemarle Hotel – where they spent the next few days reinforcing themselves with alcoholic courage, flirting with the barmaids, and spending Irene Munro's money.

Chief Inspector Mercer stated that without the information that had come from the medium Miss Groebel, allegedly under the control of Irene Munro's spirit, the murderers might never have been apprehended.

Mr Justice Avory was the judge who passed upon them the sentence of death.

The second Irene who was murdered was a maidservant named Irene Wilkins, who in December of 1921 was decoyed to Bournemouth by means of a false telegram offering her an attractive situation. Her assassin met her at the station and later assaulted her. When he had fulfilled his sadistic pleasures, he brutally murdered her, flung her body into a clump of furze bushes, and escaped from the scene without leaving any discernible clues.

In the days and weeks that followed, all investigations proved fruitless, and it seemed as though the terrible murder would have to be placed in the files marked 'unsolved'.

But then a group of Bournemouth spiritualists became interested in the case. A certain medium – remembered today only as 'Sally' – was convinced that the murderer of Irene Wilkins was still in the district. Sally gathered a number of her friends, and they visited the scene of the crime in order to pick up stronger psychic impressions. Suffused both with additional information about the murder and an increasing desire to be of assistance to the police, she wrote a letter to the local authorities that was completely ignored.

A few weeks later, however, a constable had reason to call at Sally's house regarding some trivial matter, and she boldly directed the conversation to the subject of clairvoyance. After a brief demonstration of her psychic prowess, the constable, very impressed, returned to the station house with great enthusiasm and persuaded his superiors to agree to allow a seance to take place to test Sally's abilities as a clairvoyant.

The investigating officers' scepticism vanished at the first sitting, and a series of seances was arranged in an effort to contact Irene Wilkins' spirit through Sally's mediumship.

The dead girl's clothing was brought to the medium who allowed herself to be controlled by Irene's spirit. The name 'Allaway' came through, then a complete description of a man was given. Bit by bit the whole grisly scene was reconstructed by the alleged spirit of the murdered victim.

In March 1922 Thomas Henry Allaway was arrested on a minor charge in connection with a fraudulent cheque. He was remanded, and after intense investigation by the police, he was later charged with the murder of Irene Wilkins.

Allaway was found guilty and sentenced to death by the same judge, Mr Justice Avory.

FOUNDER OF WEIRDO RELIGION GIVES SATAN A NEW NUMBER, KEEPS HIS GIRLFRIEND'S BONES IN A BUCKET

On 18 September 1989 police officers arrested Daniel Rakowitz, creator of a new religion, when they discovered a five-gallon bucket that contained the skull and bones of his twenty-six-year-old girlfriend, Monika Beerle. The grisly discovery ended a two-week search and confirmed rumours that had been circulating in New York's Lower East Side about a human body that had been dismembered and boiled.

The son of a deputy sheriff in Edna, Texas, Rakowitz, twenty-eight, with his Lone Star drawl, openly sold marijuana and amphetamines in the East Village. Described as a lanky man with scraggly hair and piercing blue eyes, he was known to his acquaintances by the live rooster he carried with him and by his long, disjointed speeches about crucifixion, reincarnation, and the power of Satan.

A busboy and musician with the splendidly appropriate name of Chris Karma spoke to the investigating officers about Rakowitz's interest in past lives and in the formation of the Church of the 966.

Rakowitz, who, according to Mr Karma, sometimes believed that he was God, explained that Satan was represented in the Bible by the number 666. In 1989, Rakowitz was certain, Satan had metamorphosed and was now represented by the number 966.

Not surprisingly, Rakowitz's girlfriend, Monika Beerle, a native of St Gallen, Switzerland, who had been studying at the Martha Graham School of Contemporary Dance, eventually grew weary of such bizarre theological prattle and asked him to move out of her apartment with his old rooster and his new religion. Angered by her lack of religious tolerance, he killed her on 19 August by 'punching her as hard as he could in the throat'. He then dismembered her body, methodically boiled away the flesh, and retained her skull and bones as mementos of their relationship.

Deputy Chief Ronald Fenrich, commander of detectives in Manhattan, stated that an investigation had begun on 8 September after the police had heard rumours about the dismemberment of a body in an apartment on East Ninth Street. On 13 September investigating officers located a woman who claimed to have seen the body. On 18 September Rakowitz was arrested and subsequently disclosed the five-gallon bucket in which he kept Monika's skeletal remains.

Rakowitz provided the police with a full videotaped confession after his arrest, while at the same time proclaiming himself to be the 'New Lord' and advocating marijuana use for everyone.

On 14 September 1990 the Texan with the shoulder-length blond hair asked that a judge empanel a jury of marijuana smokers to try him. 'That way,' he explained, 'I could get a fair trial.'

MOTHER SUED FOR FIRE DAMAGE AFTER SEX FIEND MURDERS DAUGHTER AND SETS HER ABLAZE

When Melissa Erikson of St Catherine's, Ontario, began to date John Crofutt in 1986, she really knew very little about him. He told her that he had served time in jail and that he had been released under supervised parole, but since she was a cautious woman, she scheduled a meeting with Crofutt's parole officers so that she might learn more about his criminal record.

A week before Melissa was to meet with the parole officers, Crofutt sexually assaulted and suffocated her teenaged daughter, Lori. The rape and murder took place in the basement of the townhouse that Melissa had only just rented. After Crofutt had committed the terrible deed, he poured gasoline on Lori's brutalized body and set fire to it.

Far too late to help her daughter, Melissa learned that John Crofutt had raped, choked and stabbed a woman in 1975. Then, as that earlier victim had lain helpless, befogged by pain, he burned her clothing and left her naked and unconscious in a remote field during a blizzard.

Crofutt pleaded guilty to second-degree murder in the sadistic death of Lori Erikson, and he was sentenced to life in prison with no chance for parole for fifteen years.

Late in 1989, Melissa was still adjusting to the horror of having lost a daughter to the ministrations of such a monster when she received a letter from a major insurance company in Canada advising her that they were suing her for $25,000 for the fire damage to the townhouse that had been caused by Lori's burning body.

The insurance company claimed that suing Mrs Erikson was the only way that it could get the building's insurance company to reimburse it for damage wrought inside the townhouse. But Melissa thought the company had committed the unpardonable outrage of seeking to make the family of a murder victim pay for the crime of the murderer.

The insurance suit claimed that Melissa Erikson should have known that John Crofutt 'had a propensity for setting fires' before she invited him to corent the townhouse with her. Nearly three years after the murder, their investigation had obviously uncovered the information that Crofutt had set the clothes and purse of a previous victim on fire. Such information would have been made available to Melissa Erikson at the meeting with the parole officers – if Lori's rape and murder had not occurred a week before the scheduled appointment.

When knowledge of the suit levelled against Melissa Erikson became public, hundreds of angry men and women shared her outrage.

Claudine Milby, a local director of housing, urged local nonprofit housing groups to boycott the callous insurance company. Ms Milby wondered, 'If a burglary victim was beaten up in her or his apartment and got blood all over the floor, are they going to sue the victim and make him or her pay to clean up the blood?'

The insurance company officials quietly withdrew their suit against Melissa Erikson.

THREE YEARS IN ADVANCE OF THE ACTUAL OCCURRENCE, *BORN FREE* GEORGE ADAMSON PREDICTED HIS OWN MURDER

George Adamson, Kenya's famous *Born Free* lion man, told friends in 1986 that he would one day be killed by Somali bandits, and he asked that he be buried next to the remains of Boy, his favourite lion.

Adamson and his late wife Joy received international attention after she wrote the beloved story of Elsa the lioness in the book *Born Free*. In 1966, a motion picture version of the book received Academy Awards for best original score and best title song, and in 1972 spawned a sequel, *Living Free*.

In 1986, on his eightieth birthday, Adamson told journalist David Barritt that Somali bandits would kill him, and he even posed for photographs in which he pointed out the exact spot where he wished to be buried near Boy's grave.

Adamson's personal physician also recalled that George had shared his eerie premonition with him. 'He told me that when the bandits got him,' Dr Andrew Meyerhold stated, he wanted to be buried next to Boy.'

Adamson knew that he was very unpopular with the Somalis because they held him responsible for keeping their herds from grazing on the five-hundred-square-mile area that he had staked out as a lion reserve.

On 19 August 1989 Adamson and three of his workers heard automatic weapons fire ahead of them on the road. As they rounded a bend in Adamson's Land Rover, they came upon Somali bandits, who had badly beaten one man and were about to rape a German woman tourist.

According to one of his workers, Adamson, eighty-three, appeared to give no thought for his own life, but drove straight for the Somali thugs who were ripping the clothes off the woman. The bandits opened fire with automatic rifles, killing Adamson and two other men before they fled into the bush.

Adamson had saved the woman with his last mortal act. He was laid to rest next to his beloved pet lion, Boy.

MAN WHO KILLED HIS FATHER WHEN HE WAS TWELVE IS SLAIN BY HIS OWN SON THIRTY-NINE YEARS LATER

In a bizarre twist of fate deserving of an Alfred Hitchcock motion picture or a Stephen King horror novel, a man who had shot and killed his father nearly forty years previously was shot to death by his own son in December of 1989.

Police in the Georgia city in which the tragedy occurred state that Daniel Roberts, fifty-three, was killed by five rounds from a .22-calibre hand-gun in the hands of his son, thirty-year-old Jesse Roberts, in the younger man's home.

No charges had been filed against Daniel in 1953, because the boy swore that his father had been beating his mother when he blasted him to death with a shot-gun.

In 1989, Jesse was indicted for first-degree murder after emptying his pistol into the head of his father. He claimed self-defence after having engaged in a bitter argument with Daniel.

For the benefit of the media, District Attorney Al Jenkins comments that the Roberts family were no strangers to gunshot wounds. In 1983, Daniel's brother, Mike, was shot and killed during a dispute at the County Fair. In 1983, thirty years after he murdered his father with a shot-gun, Daniel Roberts killed his next-door-neighbour, Jack Griffin, during an argument. Daniel was found guilty and sentenced to ten years in a Georgia state penitentiary, but was released in July 1988 because of prison overcrowding.

Some time after his release from prison, Daniel engaged in a series of arguments with his son. Jesse is said to have told a neighbour on the night before the killing that he was afraid that he might have to shoot his father because he wasn't going to 'take any more bull' from him.

Nancy Roberts, Jesse's wife, claimed that her husband had feared for their two children when his father forced himself into their home in a very drunken and belligerent state of mind.

Lorretta Roberts, mother of Jesse and ex-wife of Daniel, expressed her opinion that her son had been justified in killing his father. She had no doubt that Jesse acted out of fear. 'Jesse's been afraid of his daddy ever since he was a child.'

According to the former Mrs Roberts, Daniel was a 'very rough, mean person', who was mentally ill and who drank a great deal. She went on to claim that her ex-husband had beaten her and had even tried to stab her with a butcher's knife. She theorized that he might have a 'death wish' that always made him so angry.

'Maybe,' she conjectured, 'he really wanted someone to kill him, because he still felt guilty about killing his own father when he was fourteen.'

WHO LEFT THE KNIFE IN THE THROAT OF THE SEDUCTIVE OSTEOPATH?

The Kansas City police found Dr Zeo Wilkins lying on the floor of her office with a knife in her throat. Her medical gown had been ripped to shreds and her neck, throat, and forehead had been bruised and lacerated.

The office of the slain osteopath was a complete shambles. The contents of every file and desk drawer had been strewn about the room, and there had been an obvious attempt on the part of the murderer to burn the office and to cremate the corpse.

Kansas City police still have the 1919 murder in their file of unsolved crimes. Perhaps one of the reasons that they were never able to flush the real murderer out of hiding was that so many people had a good motive for killing the voluptuous vamp.

Dr Zeo Wilkins had wounded one man with her own hands and was directly responsible for the deaths of three others. She blackmailed dozens of men who had become her love slaves. She used her skill as an osteopath to mask an abortion ring for wealthy women. And as if all of the above were not enough to bring about retribution at the hands of person or persons unknown, she also peddled drugs.

For those who believe in omens, it will come as no surprise that Zeo was born the thirteenth child of poor parents who managed to eke out a living selling dairy products in Lamar, Montana. Although the Wilkins family maintained a running battle with poverty, they proudly managed to scrape up enough money for tuition when their lovely daughter declared that she wanted to go to college to become an osteopath.

The humble, God-fearing parents who scrimped and saved to put Zeo through school would have been shocked to have overheard her confession to a girlfriend: 'I want to become an osteopath because it is a profession that will bring me into intimate contact with men ... rich men. I have absolutely no compunction about using my physical charms to get just exactly what I want out of life.'

The tall, dark-haired beauty had not been enrolled in college long before she ensnared the son of a prominent banker. Zeo unabashedly wrote to a friend that she intended to marry the young man solely for the purpose of obtaining enough money from him to finance her start in osteopathy. Once she had established herself academically, she would file for divorce.

Zeo did exactly that, and when she learned that her desertion had caused the young banker to commit suicide, she displayed no remorse and barely any concern.

Zeo's diary revealed strange dialogues between her 'Zeo' self and another personality that she had named 'Helen'. It appears that she recognized her female Jekyll and Hyde personalities.

'Helen is my good self,' she wrote. 'Zeo is the evil one. My parents only know Helen. When I went away to school, I became more and more fond of Zeo. Pretty soon, I just got rid of Helen.'

Indifferent to the tragedy that she had brought about through the young banker's suicide, Zeo next set her sights on a young osteopath named C. K. Garring. Mesmerized by the dark-eyed beauty's magnetism and impressed with the brilliance of her work, he proposed to her the night after their graduation in 1905.

Garring, who was of wealthy San Antonio stock, proudly returned to his hometown with his lovely bride. They settled in the most fashionable part of the city, and Zeo soon became a popular hostess in San Antonio social circles. Life with Garring appealed to Zeo. Unfortunately for her husband, other men also had their appeal.

One night, entwined in the arms of her current lover, Zeo heard her husband's unexpected key in the lock. She grabbed a revolver from a nightstand and walked to the head of the stairs. The moment Garring opened the front door, Zeo emptied her pistol at him.

'I was all alone at home,' she later told police officers as they stood above the unconscious and bleeding osteopath who lay sprawled on his front lawn. 'I heard noises downstairs and thought that it was a burglar. I wasn't expecting my husband home until much, much later. It was an accident . . . a terrible, terrible accident!'

From Zeo's point of view, the only accident was that Garring had survived her ambush.

When he was discharged from the hospital, Garring quickly filed for divorce. Although the police had accepted Zeo's story as plausible, he had decided to take no further chances on his being 'mistaken' as a prowler by his trigger-happy wife.

Zeo accepted Garring's court charges of her being 'too hot-headed' with nary a flicker of emotion, then she moved on to Oklahoma to take a prominent banker for extravagant gifts and large sums of money. Her carpetbag stuffed with $17,000, Zeo left the careless banker to face embezzlement charges and prisoner's stripes.

The dark-haired vamp had learned a very important lesson: she didn't have to marry her victims to bleed them of their available finances. A love affair would suffice nicely and was much less messy than all those nasty divorce proceedings.

A passionate pharmacist in Kansas City was her next pick for preying. He was good for $15,000.

Zeo had carefully assessed her Junoesque figure and decided that there would be no more osteopathic bone-bending for her. She would no longer even bother to establish a practice. It was easier to milk men than to massage them.

She did find it necessary to marry her next victim, a prosperous furniture dealer named Grover Burcham.

'A marriage contract, like any other, is easily broken,' Zeo mused in her diary. 'But for the time being, I find it expedient to be married.'

Zeo went through Burcham's money with a fierce passion. Never before had she been so wantonly extravagant. Eager to please his free-spending, fiery-loving wife. Burcham tried desperately for three years to keep more in the bank than Zeo could carry in her purse. He sold his business, liquidated all his available assets, and finally resorted to burglary to keep Zeo in sufficient spending cash.

Zeo's terrible touch of death was amply demonstrated on the night that Houston police shot Burcham in the process of robbing a mansion.

The fact that she had singlehandedly brought about the complete ruination of a once-prosperous businessman even had a somewhat sobering effect on the amorous angel of destruction. Burcham's berserk campaign to satisfy her every whim had intrigued and impressed the voracious vampire. She had to admit that he was probably the only man for whom she had felt some fondness.

Zeo, true to form, had not touched any of her own money while she had been wantonly spending Burcham's entire fortune, so she decided that a luxury vacation at Colorado Springs would be the best method of curing her temporary depression. It was here that she met Thomas W. Cunningham, a retired millionaire from Joplin, Missouri.

'This is the first vacation that I've taken in more than twenty-five years,' Cunningham told the beautiful widow who had stretched her choice collection of curves next to his lawn chair. 'I'm certainly glad that I decided to take it just now or I probably never would have met you.'

Zeo assured him that somehow they would have met. Turning on the full power of her deadly dark eyes, she whispered, 'Fate has decreed that our lives should entwine.'

Soon Zeo was using her skill as an osteopath to provide Cunningham's seventy-two-year-old bones with skilled massages that stirred long-dimmed sparks into dancing flames. Hardly any time had passed before he was lavishing expensive gifts upon her and begging her to become his wife. After a discreet enquiry into how much the old man was really worth, Zeo blushed shyly and told Cunningham that he could consider the two of them one.

Cunningham gave the statuesque seductress $300,000 worth of bank stock as a wedding gift. Zeo squealed her delight and showered the elderly gentleman with kisses. Then, when his back was turned, she picked up the telephone, promptly sold his stock, and converted it into cash.

But Missouri, after all, is the 'Show-Me State', a land full of doubting Thomases, and Cunningham's friends in Joplin simply could not believe that the beautiful and sensual Zeo had married their doddering old buddy out of love. A small committee of them swooped down on the oddly matched newlyweds and literally kidnapped Cunningham from the clutching arms of his bride.

Once the elderly man was free of Zeo's seductive spell

for a time, he began to reconsider his actions. The marriage, he decided, might have been a mistake. He acquiesced to his friends' demands that he institute divorce proceedings.

When Zeo was summoned to Cunningham's lawyers, she tearfully conceded that their marital union had, perhaps, been hasty and ill advised. She insisted, however, that she truly loved the elderly banker.

For this tearful performance, the most profitable of her career, Zeo managed to wring a $456,000 settlement out of Cunningham and his attorneys.

Once the money had been securely transferred to her account, Zeo could throw discretion to the winds. She began to be seen in public with Cunningham's handsome chauffeur, Albert Marksheffel. Zeo's confidants had known that while the old man had been taking his afternoon naps alone in an upstairs bedroom, Zeo and Albert had been taking naps together in the chauffeur's quarters.

Albert, attractive, virile, but very poor, was unable to give his demanding paramour anything but love. And, for a time, that was all that the temporarily sated vampire demanded of him. She even married him and put $19,000 in his own bank account.

Although Albert could not give Zeo expensive gifts to prove his devotion, he provided odd compensation by serving as the butt of his wife's macabre sense of humour. For a time, at least, she seemed satisfied that he would provide her with laughs instead of loot.

Once Albert returned home to find their house draped in black crape. In the living room he found his wife stretched out in a coffin. In the light of dimly flickering candles, Zeo appeared to be a white-faced corpse.

Just as the fearful and confused Albert approached the casket, his mouth gaping in commingled grief and horror, Zeo sat up, shrieking at him insanely. Then, while the terrified man struggled with hysteria, his wife whooped her pleasure and merriment.

Zeo snipped the tie that bound her to Albert after two

years of matrimonial blitz. The ex-chauffeur was more delighted than depressed.

After her divorce, Zeo finally got around to a full-time career of osteopathy – with just a smattering of blackmail, abortion, and drug peddling on the side. Skillfully keeping her shady activities secret, she became one of the best-known female practitioners of osteopathy, and with her still-radiant beauty, she soon established a clientele of wealthy male patients.

But a lifetime of destroying human lives and sowing sorrow was bound to reap its malignant harvest.

'Four people have recently threatened me,' Dr Zeo Wilkins complained to her attorney. 'I'm afraid.'

To a patient, she confided: 'I have but forty-eight hours to live!'

Whether curious coincidence or terrible premonition, within two days, Zeo Wilkins lay dead with a knife in her throat.

HE ALWAYS WANTED TO BE A CRIMINAL – 'BUT NOT SUCH A BIG ONE!'

Perhaps the most frightening aspect of the serial killer is that he seldom gives any obvious indication of when he is about to perpetrate his acts of violence. One morning he may seem to be the rather prosaic person known to his friends and relatives. But by that evening he may have murdered any number of people and been transformed into a monster of incredibly vicious proportions.

To those who knew Charles Starkweather best, it seemed that the short, stocky, red-headed nineteen-year-old had only three passions: hot rods, comic books and hunting. Murder, they would have agreed, was decidedly not one of 'Little Red's' interests.

HOMICIDE

Starkweather was undersized, bandy-legged, and pigeon-toed. He usually wore cowboy boots, a black leather jacket, and blue denim trousers. He flattened tin cans and put them above the soles of his boots to add to his height.

His defective eyesight made it necessary for him to wear thick glasses. He chose to wear his red hair long and his sideburns bushy in the image of his idol, James Dean.

Charlie dropped out of high school when he was sixteen because he had developed an antagonistic attitude toward formal education. For a time, he drove a garbage truck, but he was fired for sitting behind the wheel of the vehicle and shouting obscenities and insults at passing strangers.

Although he was known to be moody and unpredictable, and possessed a violent temper that often led him into fights with much larger and older men, no one would have predicted that Charlie would, in January 1958, begin a trail of slaughter that would leave ten corpses in his wake and throw the entire state of Nebraska into a panic. Before it was over, Governor Victor Anderson would mobilize two hundred troops of the National Guard to aid the thousand-man posse of the sheriff's office. Plans were formulated for a house-to-house search in Lincoln, a city with a population of nearly one hundred thousand.

In spite of the veritable legions of law enforcement officers engaged in an around-the-clock pursuit of Charles Starkweather and his fourteen-year-old girlfriend, the pair of fugitives managed to avoid the more than one hundred roadblocks set up by the safety patrol and cross the state line into Wyoming.

The grisly odyssey of carnage began when Charlie shot his girlfriend's parents, then pinned a note on their door that told folks to stay away because 'Everybody is sick with the Flue'. After the murder of the family, the two young lovers just sat around the house watching television for three or four days before they decided to run away.

Why had he killed his girlfriend's family?

According to Charlie, he had just been sitting around the

Bartlett house while his sweetie was still in school. They got tired of him hanging around, so he just told them what they could do about it.

Mrs Bartlett got mad and hit him, so he had to hit her back. Then Mr Bartlett started to come for him, so he had to let both of them have it with his rifle. The baby he killed later while his girlfriend was watching television.

Detailing some of his other killings, Charlie said that he had murdered one young couple so he could take their car. He shot a farmer because he had a gun that Charlie wanted to take with him. The family in Lincoln had been slaughtered after the two fugitives had used their home for a while as a hideout. Yet another man had been killed to obtain another automobile.

Starkweather had finally been apprehended in a chase at speeds of up to 115 miles per hour. Sheriff Earl Heflin blasted the rear window out of the stolen Packard, and Charlie finally braked to a tyre-squealing halt in the middle of the highway four miles out of Douglas, Nebraska.

Little Red staggered out of the bullet-riddled Packard, whimpering in pain and holding both hands to his right ear. 'I'm hit,' he wailed. 'You lousy bastards shot me!'

While Sheriff Heflin held a shot-gun on Starkweather, Police Chief Robert Ainsley examined the wound. 'You're a real tough guy, aren't you?' Ainsley snorted. 'You've got a superficial cut caused by flying glass.'

During their interrogation of the pint-sized murderer, one of the officers asked the most important question of all: why had he committed the murders?

Little Red had an answer. 'I always wanted to be a criminal,' he said solemnly, then added, 'But not this big a one.'

HE MADE A GRAVESIDE VOW THAT HE WOULD FIND HIS SON'S KILLERS

Joe Viscido, Jr., a twenty-seven-year-old Florida surfing champion, had unwisely undergone a brief experiment with drugs, and in the fall of 1986, he was doing his best to straighten out his life.

But on the night of 12 October, two men burst into his home in Deerfield Beach, Florida, to steal cocaine that they believed had been stored there. Mercilessly, the two thugs beat Joe, then shot him in the head.

When the scum who killed Joe Viscido, Jr. snuffed out the young man's life, they didn't know that there was a Joe Viscido, Sr. who would go to the ends of the earth to track down his son's executioners. The heartbroken used-car dealer from Pompano Beach stood beside his son's coffin and made a vow that he would track down whoever had murdered him.

When the original police investigation was unable to produce any substantial leads, Joe, fifty-nine, closed his car lot, converted his van into a camper, and began to spend his nights parked outside the houses of suspected drug dealers.

Joe told his wife that there was a good chance that he would be killed, but he felt that he must do everything he could to avenge their son's death. They both knew that Joe, Jr. had had some problems, but he had been working hard to straighten himself out. He had not deserved to die such a violent death at the hands of drug pushers.

For the next four years, Joe, Sr., slowly pieced together shreds of evidence, and he spent over $30,000 on his lonely, relentless crusade. He literally camped outside the houses of alleged drug dealers. He rigorously copied down licence plate numbers of suspicious vehicles, then paid private investigators to find out who owned the cars. He donned disguises, wore wigs, and often switched automobiles to avoid detection by those he was hunting.

From the outset, Joe knew that he was up against a really bad gang, but his grief more than outweighed his fear. Sergeant William Murray of the Broward County Sheriff's Department told the press that he had been greatly concerned for the health and the welfare of Joe Viscido, Sr. 'I knew the kind of people that he was dealing with, but it was his perseverance that put the case over the edge.'

Joe's incessant digging and his tireless efforts of surveillance managed to get the investigation into the circumstances of his son's death reactivated. And this time when the homicide detectives interviewed a few more witnesses, they found they had hit pay dirt. Three alleged drug dealers were sent to jail to await trial for the brutal execution slaying of Joe Viscido, Jr.

Joe, Sr.'s current mission is the formation of a national group that will be designed to assist friends and relatives of crime victims to learn the best methods of assisting the police in their investigations into the terrible acts of violence that cost so many lives.

THE BELCH THAT COST A LIFE

The terrible feud had begun with a belch.

Twenty-four-year-old James Hagarty's relationship with his girlfriend Nancy had been steadily deteriorating when he called her apartment in March 1991, to discuss their problems. It would be good, he thought, to air their differences and to get their romance back on track.

Nancy's girlfriend answered the telephone, but her boyfriend Bruce Cascio grabbed the receiver, burped into the mouthpiece, and hung up.

A few minutes later, a furious James Hagarty arrived at

the apartment, kicked in the door, and demanded to know who had burped on the telephone.

Cascio readily admitted that he was the party responsible for the belch, and the two young men began to fight.

Over the following weeks, the men continued to argue and to assault one another at every available opportunity.

Finally, on 17 April, while Cascio was in the process of hitting Hagarty's car with a baseball bat, Hagarty shot and killed him.

'He started it by burping,' Hagarty testified at his trial. 'He stuck his nose into my business.'

TWO ANGRY DISCIPLES DECREE: NO MORE TEMPTATIONS FOR JESUS, AS THEY BLOW HIM TO KINGDOM COME WITH DYNAMITE

On the evening of 10 December 1958, Krishna Venta, the new incarnation of Jesus Christ, resplendent in his yellow robe, strode boldly out into the foyer of the Fountain of the World administration building to meet his two accusers.

'Muller and Kamenoff!' he bellowed at them. 'You are instruments of the devil. You were sent to disrupt our organization and sway us from the path of righteousness. You deserve to die!'

'*And you,*' Ralph Muller retorted, '*are going to die!*'

After pronouncing the death sentence upon his former master, Muller produced a neatly tied bundle of dynamite, its fuse and cap already intact.

Krishna Venta's eyes moved anxiously from the explosives to the faces of his dissident disciples. 'You can't kill me,' he argued. 'I am Christ himself!'

'You are an evil Christ who takes our money and our wives!' Peter Kamenoff shouted, challenging the man's professed divinity.

Kamenoff was clearly one disciple who had had enough of the self-ordained, self-resurrected messiah who stood so defiantly before them. He flicked his cigarette lighter and held its sputtering flame to the fuse on the bundle of dynamite that Muller held.

Krishna Venta refused to believe the scenario that was taking place in the foyer of the administration building of the Fountain of the World religious movement. 'I have Providence to protect me,' he proclaimed, perhaps as much to reassure himself as his rebellious followers. 'Surely you realize that I cannot die.'

The mystic had long since persuaded his followers that in 1932 he had teleported himself to the United States from the Valley of the Masters below Mount Everest in Nepal. He had lived in Nepal for centuries, having originally arrived on earth in a spaceship from the planet Neophrates. He had told his disciples that he was ageless.

Muller held the explosives for one small, decisive moment, almost as if he were seriously considering that he and Kamenoff might be wrong and that this man was indeed the Christ. But any last doubts were blotted out for ever when the dynamite went off. The two-storey administration building of the Fountain of the World cult disintegrated, and along with it, Krishna Venta, his two assassins, and seven other members of the cult.

What had prompted these two once loyal and devout members of the Fountain of the World to commit such an atrocity against their religious mentor?

As is so often the case with too many cult leaders, Krishna Venta had failed in his relationships with his own subjects. Greed and sexual promiscuity had ensnared him and made him heedless of personal danger. Tragically, he had come to believe his own pronouncements that he was truly what he proclaimed to be – and just as invincible.

Krishna Venta, as the new incarnation of Jesus Christ, gave birth to himself in 1951, after long, arduous troubles with the law and a long string of failures in other endeavours. The messiah had been born in San Francisco in 1911 under the 'earth name' of Francis Heindswaltzer Pencovic, and it was under that name that he had studied theology.

In 1941, while living under his middle name in Phoenix, Arizona, he was held and questioned by the police for allegedly writing a threatening letter to President Franklin Delano Roosevelt.

Later, he transformed himself to 'Frank Jensen' and committed a number of petty thefts and burglaries. It was some time after he had been placed in a hospital for psychiatric evaluation that he received the supernatural word that he should metamorphose himself once again – this time into Krishna Venta.

Once he had convinced himself that he was the 'only-begotten son of God', it didn't take him long to convince others of his divine credentials. It seemed that in no time at all he had ordained a priesthood composed of donors to the cause of the Fountain of the World, refusing admittance only to those who did not come bearing gifts. Beautiful women, however, could enter by virtue of their physical attributes.

A benefactor's large donation enabled the Fountain of the World to purchase twenty-six acres in beautiful Box Canyon, about forty-five miles north west of Los Angeles. In the early 1950s, a nonprofit corporation was formed in California with Krishna Venta as president. Under him were twelve disciples. All applicants were technically required to bequeath to the Fountain of the World all earthly wealth that they possessed – a sort of salvation credit plan.

From the beginning, Krishna Venta was determined not to be run out of the state by the authorities. He earnestly set about creating good public relations, training his followers in disaster aid and other socially helpful fields.

Of most worthy note was the skill of the Fountain of the World cultists as firefighters. Timber fires in that section of California were a menace, and when one would be reported,

Krishna Venta, at the command of his brigade, would speed to the scene in his station wagon to supervise the construction of firebreaks and trenches to combat the blaze.

As noble as all this might seem, what probably caused the messiah's downfall was his penchant for racing to the fires in the company of young, beautiful, female disciples. His was a collegian's dream. He had the back end of his station wagon outfitted with a mattress and all the other necessities of lovemaking. Whenever there was a break in the fire fighting, Krishna Venta would steal away with a lovely disciple to 'restore his blood circulation'.

The doctrine of the Fountain of the World allowed its members the unrestrained use of tobacco or alcohol, but it ordered a tight rein on their sexual desires. It was not, of course, that Krishna Venta was against sex, but he did most heartily wish to keep the cult's personal expression of sexual activity away from the unfavourable scrutiny of the public eye. He did not wish rumours of orgies and 'free love' to excite his more conservative neighbours and thus upset his going concern.

Most of the true believers went along with the cult's rules and got married before they engaged in any serious or regular sexual intercourse. As one might suppose, as the spiritual master of the Fountain of the World, Krishna Venta reserved the right to dally with whichever women he chose. On occasion, his sexual indulgence was cloaked under the guise of various subterfuges, some religious and some therapeutic. Most often, however, he simply willed into bed a host of mistresses.

Krishna Venta's image as a perfect saviour began to melt. He went to Las Vegas and lost a great deal of money at the crap tables, claiming that he had done so only to see how the sinners conducted themselves in that city of glaring neon lights and clattering slot machines.

He travelled to London on a missionary tour, but reports reached his followers that even though the British had given him a cool reception, he stayed in expensive hotels and lived in the grand style, as if he were a visiting rajah.

Once back home in Box Canyon, he continued to eat nothing but the finest foods while his disciples were left to scrounge for themselves.

It is no wonder, then, that his annoyed followers began to question the validity of his messiahship.

The spiritual straw that broke the faithful's back was Krishna Venta's unscrupulous use of women for his own pleasures. Muller and Kamenoff had learned that both of their wives had been summoned to their guru's private orgies in the back of the infamous station wagon. Such knowledge proved to be more than they could endure, and it became the catalytic element that brought them to the door of the Fountain of the World's administration building on that fateful December evening.

Together, the two disappointed disciples joined their master on a one-way trip to Kingdom Come.

MINDREADER'S STARING CONTEST WITH MASS MURDERER PRODUCES HIDDEN MURDER WEAPON

On 9 July 1928 news of a grisly mass murder committed in a farm home rocked the countryside of Mannville, Alberta, Canada.

Dr Harley Heaslip was summoned to the Henry Booher farm by Vernon, the man's twenty-one-year-old son. The doctor was shocked to discover the bodies of Mrs Henry Booher, her son Fred, and two hired men – all of whom had been shot to death.

According to Henry Booher, he, his two teenaged daughters, and Vernon had left the farm shortly after supper to attend a basketball game in Mannville. They had returned to find a nightmarish scene of bloody carnage.

Constable Frederick Olsen of the Royal Canadian Mounted Police, Alberta Division, was assigned to investigate the grisly murders. From the location of the mortal wounds and the distribution of the bodies, Constable Olsen determined that Mrs Booher had been the main target.

For one thing, she was the only victim who had been shot in the back of the head. Fred Booher, her son, had taken several shots fired at point-blank range into his face. It appeared to the constable that the young man must have come running at the sound of the shots that had killed his mother, only to be gunned down as he reached the kitchen door.

The two hired hands, Gromby and Rosyk, were probably killed because they had recognized the murderer – or so Constable Olsen deduced. All the evidence strongly suggested either a member of the Booher family, or someone well known to them, as the killer. The law officer bemoaned the lack of the murder weapon, which, from the evidence obtained from the autopsies, was a .30-calibre rifle.

As he conducted routine enquiries in Mannville, Constable Olsen learned that Vernon was seriously dating a girl of whom his mother did not approve. The young woman, aware of Mrs Booher's hostility towards her, finally broke off the relationship with Vernon. Increasingly, the investigator was becoming more and more convinced that the twenty-one-year-old man had killed his mother, his brother, and the two hired hands.

Even though he had no trace of the murder weapon, the constable decided to confront the young man with a direct accusation of murder.

'Have you found the rifle?' Vernon responded in a cool manner, totally devoid of emotion. 'Do you have any evidence to back up such an accusation against me?'

Constable Olsen was sickened by the youth's complete lack of contrition. He became even more determined to win a confession from the young man with ice water in his veins.

Vernon Booher was charged with the murder of his

mother, his brother, and the family's two employees. He was taken to Provincial Police headquarters in Edmonton, Alberta. Officers there advised the young man that he might as well confess.

'That's what you think!' he replied with mocking laughter.

Inspector Hancock of the Alberta Provincial Police knew that he had a difficult case on his hands. The hard-hearted Vernon was only too aware that the police could not gain a conviction without a confession – and wringing a confession out of him seemed impossible without the evidence of a murder weapon. Once they had the rifle that had slaughtered four people in the Mannville farm home, they could try for fingerprints on the barrel or stock.

The situation had clearly reached an impasse until the night that Inspector Hancock read about a mind reader in his evening paper. The man, Maximillian Langsner, lived in Vancouver, and from all accounts, certainly appeared to be the genuine article – not a phoney fortune-teller or a clever stage mentalist.

The inspector had never indulged in unorthodox police procedures, but at this point in the frustrating investigation, he was willing to try anything. He picked up the telephone and put in a call to Langsner.

The thirty-five-year-old psychic accepted the inspector's invitation to Edmonton to attempt to solve the murders, and he arrived two days later.

Eager to be taken seriously, the dapper, well-dressed, articulate Langsner attempted to explain his beliefs regarding telepathy and mind reading and to elaborate on how there mental abilities could be employed in solving criminal cases. Langsner's descriptions of the human mind sending out electrical impulses that other minds, specially trained, could learn to intercept and to read, had Inspector Hancock reconsidering his initial impulse to contact the young mystic.

After additional discussions, however, Langsner convinced the police officials that he was qualified to attempt to probe Vernon Booher's mind and to learn where he had hidden the murder weapon. Early one afternoon, Langsner sat on a chair that he had placed outside of Vernon's cell and began to stare at the suspect intensely.

For the first few hours, Booher ignored the mentalist. But by the fourth hour, Vernon had begun to sweat. The prisoner broke his contemptuous silence and started to swear at his dapper observer, but Langsner continued to stare, unruffled.

Five hours after the 'staring contest' had begun, Vernon Booher dropped in exhaustion to his cot. His eyes floated toward Langsner's and the two men locked eyes. Langsner quietly stood up, leaving Vernon to fall into a deep sleep.

Within a few moments, Langsner summoned Inspector Hancock. 'The rifle which you seek is hidden in a clump of bushes five hundred or six hundred feet from the farmhouse,' he reported. 'Let me have a pencil and paper.'

While Hancock watched over the telepath's shoulder, Langsner drew a sketch of the Booher farm – which he had never *physically* seen – a clump of bushes and two trees, one tree about half-way between the house and the bushes, the other tree just beyond the bushes.

When the two men arrived at the Booher farm, the trees and bushes were just as Langsner had depicted them. He ran towards the clump of bushes, fumbled around for a few moments, then triumphantly held aloft a .303 British rifle.

On the basis of this discovery – and the evidence obtained from a few more sessions with the telepath – Vernon Booher broke down and confessed the terrible crime. He had been consumed with hatred for his mother after she had been instrumental in breaking up his love affair. He had resolved to kill her. His brother and the two other men had been shot to eliminate any witness to the murder.

Booher was convicted of the murders, and he died on the gallows.

CHAPTER SEVEN

HUMAN SACRIFICE

THE TEENAGERS CHOSE JENNIFER TO BE THE SACRIFICIAL LAMB ON SATAN'S ALTAR OF EVIL

When the police in the small Louisiana town picked up the three teenagers from Georgia, in the wee hours of a January morning in 1988, they were inclined to be lenient towards the kids. True, a plate check showed that the van had been reported stolen, but Fred Goodman, James Frost, and Kristi Callan claimed that they had just borrowed Jimmy's family van for a little vacation time in New Orleans. They were not criminals, just teenagers looking for a good time.

On the other hand, the senior Frost's complaint suggested that the teenagers had not taken the van with parental permission, so the authorities felt they had no choice other than to detain the teenagers until they heard from James' parents.

Later that day, Sergeant Rick Heath received word from a female inmate at the county jail who said that she must speak with him. Heath knew the woman as an informant who had helped the police solve a number of cases. She had been arrested for loitering and had shared a jail cell with Kristi Callan, the teenager from Georgia.

The informant told Heath that Kristi had said that she and another girl had been picked up by two guys who took them to a deserted farmhouse. The kids had all got high on grass, listened to heavy metal, drank blood, worshipped Satan – and then sacrificed the other girl!

The street-smart informant said that the sweet teenager from Georgia with the pretty smile had really scared her.

Heath later told Major Bob Peters the incredible story, adding that he knew the informant and trusted her. 'She was scared. She really believes those kids performed a human sacrifice,' he said.

A crime check revealed only that Goodman had a few prior arrests on misdemeanour charges. Frost and Kristi Callan both had clean records – but the police did learn that Kristi had recently been sent to a juvenile home and that she and three other girls were listed as runaways. Two of the girls had returned, but Kristi and a sixteen-year-old named Jennifer Reynolds were on the records as still missing.

The police in Louisiana saw no reason to charge Kristi with auto theft. She had merely been a hitchhiker picked up by Goodman and Frost, so she was released on her own recognizance.

It was after Goodman and Frost had been flown back to Georgia that Sheriff Bill Hankins read Sergeant Heath's report, then followed his gut instinct and managed to get Goodman to reveal a terrible crime of satanic human sacrifice. Sheriff Hankins simply started speaking about satanism in a general, almost casual, manner, and Goodman, who had previously been tight lipped, suddenly became animated and talkative.

The teenager admitted that he had been a member of a satanic cult for a year. He told the sheriff that he had just been a regular high school kid until he had met a woman who had got his attention with promises of power and sex, then informed him that she was a satanic witch.

Goodman went on to tell how he had begun to meet regularly with the satanist. They would listen to heavy metal music and read from the *Satanic Bible*. Soon, he had himself become a practicing satanist and was participating in the sacrifice of animals and the drinking of their blood.

Proudly, he told how he had risen in the ranks to become

the high priest of his own coven. 'I had followers. I had power. It was neat!'

Eventually, the persistent Sheriff Hankins had the whole sordid story. James Frost was a member of Goodman's coven. When they picked up the two runaway girls, they discovered that Kristi had already dabbled in satanism and that she was more than willing to accept Goodman as her high priest.

Goodman and Frost had grown bored performing animal sacrifices and blood rituals, and they had discussed a human sacrifice for quite some time. Kristi voted in favour of the idea, and the three of them decided that Jennifer would make a perfect offering to Satan.

After working themselves into a killing fever on grass and heavy music in the upstairs bedroom of the abandoned farmhouse, they looped a leather shoelace around Jennifer's neck and took turns tightening it.

When they knew that she was dead, they read from the *Satanic Bible* and chanted over her body, hoping that their sacrifice would enable Satan to materialize before them.

The media made a great deal of Goodman's jailhouse conversion to Christianity and his recanting of satanism; but during his trial in May 1988, he seemed to relate his career as a demonic cultist with great gusto and enthusiasm. He told of slaughtering large numbers of dogs, cats, and chickens to Satan and of drinking their blood and eating their eyeballs and intestines.

Goodman testified that he had received 'power' for performing such rituals. Satan had rewarded him with 'money, sex, drugs – anything I wanted'.

Wearing a cross around his neck, Goodman pleaded guilty to murder and received an automatic life sentence. He also agreed to testify against his former follower, James Frost.

In June 1988, Frost was also sentenced to life imprisonment. Kristi Callan was found guilty of being an accessory to murder and was sentenced to a three-year prison term.

THEY TOOK A PROSTITUTE FROM THE STREETS AND MADE HER – MEXICO'S PERVERSE PRIESTESS OF HUMAN SACRIFICE

In a coastal province in Mexico in 1961, the Federal Police discovered that members of a bizarre cult had sacrificed twelve persons to the dark gods. Hearts had been ripped from the bodies of living victims during grisly ceremonies. Others had been stoned to death on orders from a prostitute turned 'goddess'.

Rosenda Cavallo was just a prostitute who prowled the bars of Mexico City for paying customers. Then, in the summer of 1960, fate dealt Rosenda a very strange hand, and in the span of a few months, she had performed human sacrifices offered to ancient Mayan gods, conducted a sex cult, and become a high priestess who offered her followers a ceremonial goblet filled with a mixture of marijuana leaves and human blood. It was the Cervantez brothers, Jose and Orlando, who presented Rosenda and her brother Fausto with a most unusual proposition: they needed a god and a goddess to enliven the sex cult they had established in a small farming village near the coast.

Jose outlined the scam to Rosenda and her homosexual brother, who had pimped his sister's flesh since they had been children.

For several months, Jose explained, the two brothers had been living in a cave, holding mystic rites and promising the farmers that if they brought them regular offerings of money, they would continue to pray to the cave gods and convince them to give up the supposed treasure that the Incas had buried in the mountains.

At first all had gone well. The farmers brought their money, and they had convinced the villagers that sex with the priests was necessary to rid their bodies of demons.

Next, when the farmers and their wives desired something more, Jose and Orlando initiated a beautiful village girl to serve as a priestess. Her voluptuous figure and her nude dances had kept the men's desires off the treasure for several weeks.

But now the villagers had really become impatient. They complained that they had grown weary of purging their bodies of demons. They were now demanding their share of the treasure. In a last desperate effort to keep the villagers' minds off the treasure, the Cervantez brothers had promised them the reincarnation of a local faith healer who had been dead for fifty years.

'In the eyes of the villagers,' Jose explained, 'she has become a goddess. We have promised them that she will return to them in the company of a Mayan god. Even now, we are supposed to be up on the mountaintop praying for their holy arrival. We decided that it would be to our greater advantage to come to Mexico City to seek someone such as yourselves.'

Rosenda's sense of the dramatic was given full expression when she and Fausto appeared in the sacred cave in a puff of billowing smoke. When the 'holy mists' cleared, the villagers fell in awe before the forms of the reincarnated faith healer and the ancient Mayan god.

Rosenda informed the villagers that before she could once again perform healings or the treasure could be revealed, there must be a serious purging of their lusts and their bodily demons.

After a time, however, there were once again rumblings of discontent. Inevitably, the day had to come when marijuana and group sex could no longer distract the poor villagers' thoughts of ending their poverty with the promised treasure.

That night the 'goddess' told the group assembled in the cave that while it was true that most of them had been faithful, there existed among them those who had profaned the priests and the gods. 'It is these doubters who are keeping the gold from you,' she screamed at them, 'not the gods!'

Rosenda told them that it was, indeed, the gods' wish

that the villagers should be happy. But the gods would not release their ancient gold into the hands of those who doubted. Alas, all of them must suffer because of the lack of faith of a few.

A confused babble arose as the villagers loudly proclaimed their devotion to the gods. At a signal from Rosenda, two men were pushed into the centre of the circle.

These were the unbelievers, she shouted above the gasps of surprise and the whimpers of fear. These were the pigs who had denied the old gods and their priests. The guilt lay not with the others, but with these dogs!

Rosenda was swift in her judgement: the unbelievers must be killed or the gods would never release the gold of the ancient kingdom!

Without hesitation, the blonde goddess commanded the two men to be stoned and their blood collected in basins for group communion.

And thus it was that Rosenda Cavallo had created a method by which to guarantee the scam a longer life at the expense of a few villagers' lives. She had discovered that dissent might be dealt with in that most ancient and time-tested method – human sacrifice.

By 1 June 1961, at least eight villagers had been slaughtered by Rosenda's primitive and direct manner of cult purification. But also by that time, those men and women who guessed that they might be marked for sacrifice had begun fleeing the accursed village.

The Cervantez brothers and Fausto all voted to terminate the con at once and head back to Mexico City before the authorities learned of their cult. Rosenda, however, decided that what the cult really needed to survive was one great and dramatic act on the part of the priesthood. She would offer a lovely village girl in an elaborately staged sacrifice.

But fate was about to deal Rosenda a wild card. At the most terrible moment of the ritual murder, perhaps the only citizen in the village who did not know about the god and the goddess of the cave happened to walk by and witness the vicious sacrifice of the girl.

Each day during the school year, teenaged Juan Navarro rose before dawn so that he might walk the seventeen miles to a small, one-room schoolhouse. With such a schedule to keep, young Juan had not even heard a whisper about group sex and ritual sacrifices. But now, all at once, he was witnessing a scene out of humankind's savage past.

After the girl had been beaten to a bloody, faceless corpse by ceremonial clubbing, a villager Juan recognized stepped forward and shouted something about now wanting the gold at once. A woman in ceremonial robes screamed at him for being an unbeliever and commanded the others to slash out his heart with machetes.

While the teenager watched the gory act with horror-widened eyes, the villagers hacked open the chest of the man and ripped out his still-beating heart.

Somehow, Juan managed to run the seventeen miles to a police station in a complete state of shock. Patrolman Alfredo Cerrito did not scoff at the boy's terrible story. He had been hearing some very strange tales about a pagan sex and drug cult flourishing in the small farming village.

Patrolman Cerrito returned to the village with the teenager to investigate the allegations. Tragically, the cultists fell upon the officer and the boy, chopped them to death with machetes, and offered their corpses as sacrifice to the Mayan gods.

Inspector Gaspar Barrios did not repeat the patrolman's fatal error. Although the cultists resisted arrest and fired upon Barrios and his officers, they surrendered when their immortal priest, Jose Cervantez, caught a bullet from a policeman's carbine and died instantly.

Only eleven days after their arrest, Fausto and Rosenda Cavallo were brought to trial along with twelve members of the cult.

Although the Mexican state in which the murders were committed had abolished capital punishment, each of the fourteen cultists brought to trial received the maximum sentence of thirty years in the state prison.

CHAPTER EIGHT

KIDNAPPING

SIGN THIS KID UP TO STRIKE OUT CRIME! HIS BULL'S-EYE PITCHING HELPS NAB A KIDNAPPER

When teenaged Jason Michaels first heard the screams coming from the desert, he was afraid that his little sister Janice was in trouble.

Jason, who lives with his divorced mother in an Arizona desert community, was visiting his father in a nearby city in October of 1989. He had just walked out of the backyard when the terrible cries for help set him running in the direction of the disturbance.

As he looked toward the desert, he saw a man struggling with a teenaged girl. Although the girl was doing her best to keep her assailant's hands from her throat, he was dragging her further into the desert. It seemed apparent to Jason that the man intended to strangle her.

At first Jason didn't know what to do. He knew he had to help the girl, but how? He was only a kid, probably no match for the brute who was assaulting the girl. But he could see that the creep was really hurting her.

Jason spotted some rocks on the ground about the size of baseballs, and sudden inspiration flooded his brain. Although the scumbag was at least seventy-five feet way, Jason knew that he had to go for it. He scooped up one of the rocks and threw it at the strangler with all of his might.

The rock hit the sleeze in the back, but it didn't seem to bother him.

With grim determination, Jason picked up another rock, and another. In rapid succession, three more rocks thudded into the slimeball's back.

'That's when he suddenly let go of the girl,' Jason said later. 'He turned around to look at me like he was going to come after me, but then he turned back to chase the girl.'

Jason felt his heart sink. He had stopped the kidnapper for a moment, but now the man was returning to his awful deed. Jason was confused, desperate. But then he heard the sound of heavy footsteps thudding near him.

Jason's father and a neighbour had heard the girl's screams and were rushing past him to come to her rescue. In moments, they had caught the man, and they held him until the police arrived.

Later, after Nicholas Sanders, a transient, had been charged with kidnapping in the case, it was learned that he had approached the thirteen-year-old girl on the street and told her that he was an undercover cop. Sanders' story was that he needed her help in a drug bust, and he talked her into accompanying him outside of town. Once they had arrived in the desert area near the Michaels home, the girl had become suspicious of the 'policeman' and had tried to run away. That was when he had begun to strangle her.

Investigating police officers stated that there was no question that Jason's on-target pitching had delayed the kidnapper. The teenager's four direct hits had distracted Sanders and had given his father and a neighbour a chance to catch him and to hold him until the police arrived.

The local police department and a veterans' group presented Jason Michaels with awards for bravery. The modest teenager only expressed his surprise at how well he had thrown those rocks. He'd had no idea that his pitching arm was so good.

WEIRD KIDNAPPINGS AND MURDERS WITHOUT CORPSES!

Among the weirdest of the weird crimes are those instances of strange and mysterious disappearances that appear so much to be apparent kidnappings or homicides – but never produce a body or a suspect.

Whenever a large number of people disappear in one particular location over a period of time, the police investigators are left with the disturbing enigma of whether they are dealing with a 'Jack the Ripper', who manages to dispose of the *corpus dilecti*, a kidnapper, who carries the victims to some faraway place to dispose of them, or some unknown perverse monster out of *A Nightmare on Elm Street* or *Friday the 13th*.

In the period from November 1945 to December 1950, seven people disappeared in the Mt Glastenbury region near Bennington, Vermont. There are no records of any disappearances in that area before 1945, and the strange vanishing ended according to some undetermined timetable after 1950. But some area residents still warn hikers to keep a wary eye out for murderers, monsters, or aliens from UFOs.

Middie Rivers, the first person to vanish from Mt Glastenbury, seemed a most unlikely candidate to become lost for an hour, let alone for ever. Rivers was a seventy-five-year old hunting guide who knew the region as thoroughly as any man alive. On 12 November 1945, Rivers led four hunters into the mountain region and then, while returning to camp a bit ahead of the other men, disappeared completely.

Within hours of his disappearance, hundreds of volunteers and local and state police began to scour the area. The search was continued for a month without the discovery of even the slightest trace of the missing guide.

The strange disappearance of Middie Rivers had just

enough time to become a part of the local legends when attractive Paula Weldon, an eighteen-year-old student at Bennington College, set off on a hike on 1 December 1946. While on her trek, Paula was seen by a number of fellow students, a gas station attendant, a local building contractor, and a janitor of the Bennington Banner Building. But then the teenager walked on to hike into oblivion.

State and local police were soon supplemented in their search for the missing girl by state detectives and the FBI. Hundreds of volunteer searchers assisted in a meticulous exploration of the region. Journalists tracked down supposed leads that took them to Canada, even to the West Indies. But no one found a single thread from Paula's coat or a single hair from her head.

The third disappearance in Mt Glastenbury occurred on the third anniversary of Paula Weldon's apparent evaporation into nowhere. On 1 December 1949 James E. Tetford vanished in a manner even more peculiar than the two previous victims of whoever or whatever it is that goes hunting on Mt Glastenbury.

Tetford had been visiting relatives in South Albans, Vermont, and he had decided to return to the Soldiers' Home in Bennington. He boarded a bus, found a seat, bade farewell to his relatives – but he was never seen to leave the bus and he never returned to the Soldiers' Home.

An exhaustive investigation could reveal absolutely no clues to Tetford's strange disappearance. Several people had seen him board the bus, but no one could remember having seen him get off the vehicle.

It would seem to be impossible to exit a bus *en route* to its next station, either voluntarily or involuntarily, without being seen by the other passengers or the bus driver. Yet somehow James E. Tetford had apparently managed that impossible feat – or he had mysteriously been removed by a person or persons unknown.

On 12 October 1950, eight-year-old Paul Jepson was left on the seat of a truck while his father stepped a few feet

KIDNAPPING

away to perform a small errand. Moments later, when Mr Jepson returned to the cab of his truck, he found that his son had vanished.

As in the previous disappearances, hundreds of volunteers were mobilized to supplement the state and local law enforcement agencies, and well-trained bloodhounds were set on the trail.

Was it only an eerie coincidence that the hounds lost the scent of Paul Jepson at the exact spot where Paula Weldon had last been seen? When the dogs came to this precise spot, they could only mill about in confusion and bay despairingly.

Two weeks later, an experienced woodswoman and expert gun handler named Frieda Langer disappeared while on a hike in the Glastenbury woods with her cousin, Herbert Elsner. Mrs Langer was thoroughly familiar with the area, but her knowledge of the woods did not assist her any more than the outdoors expertise of Middie Rivers had helped him to evade the fate of a strange disappearance.

Frieda Langer had slipped and fallen in a shallow stream at about 4:30 p.m. She told Elsner that she would quickly run home, change clothes, and rejoin him.

The man waited in the woods for an hour, then decided to return to see what had delayed his cousin. He was horrified to learn that she had not been seen to emerge from the woods at all.

Volunteers trudged through the snow-covered woods of Glastenbury for a month before they called off the search. No one could believe that the woodswise Frieda Langer could have become lost, but the authorities knew that they had expertly and systematically covered every foot of the forest.

Only a few days after the officials had terminated the search for Mrs Langer, Frances Christman left home to visit a friend who lived but a half-mile away. Somewhere on that brief winter's eve stroll, the woman vanished without a trace.

No one could blame the weary volunteers and official searchers and trackers for beginning to talk of culprits and kidnappers with more than conventional human abilities for having been somehow responsible for the strange disappearances. At the same time, the terror of the prospect of possibly becoming a future victim of the mysterious force at work in the region of Mt Glastenbury began to seep into the consciousness of the area residents.

And then it was learned that yet another unfortunate hiker had vanished and that she had actually preceded Frances Christman in her walk into oblivion.

Martha Jeanette Jones had disappeared on 6 November, but her mother had not notified the authorities of the teenager's absence because she feared that Martha had run off with a soldier stationed in Virginia. When at last Mrs Jones had discovered that the young man truthfully knew nothing of her daughter's whereabouts, a massive search was begun in the haunted Mt Glastenbury area on 12 December. After another exhaustive combing of the region, it had to be decreed that sixteen-year-old Martha had joined the other victims in whatever limbo had claimed them.

Although Martha Jones was the seventh and last person to disappear in the Mt Glastenbury area in this perverse period of mysterious vanishings, there is a bizarre footnote that must be added.

On 12 May 1951, seven months after her disappearance, the corpse of Frieda Langer suddenly appeared in such an open, easily visible area of the forest that it seemed totally unbelievable that hundreds of searchers could have overlooked it during the month-long scouring of the woods.

The physical remains of Mrs Langer were the only ones ever discovered, and exposure to the elements had left the corpse in such a condition as to render detection of violence or any other kind of clue to her fate virtually impossible.

In none of the other cases of strange disappearances on Mt Glastenbury was there even a single thread of clothing or strand of hair that could be traced to any of the six

KIDNAPPING 87

victims. No motive for murder could be determined in any of the seven cases. No ransom demands were ever received by any of the victims' families. No clues were ever found to explain the total disappearance of the victims, and with the exception of Mrs Langer's corpse, not a single trace of any of them was ever discovered.

When the Azusa, California, police took the call about the two kids who had disappeared on that Sunday morning, 6 August 1956, the authorities feared that they had a case of child molestation and kidnapping on theirs hands. But they, too, like the officials in Mt Glastenbury, soon learned that they were dealing with a crime with no bodies and no perpetrator. In fact, they would find themselves confronting a forest of disappearing children.

Thirteen-year-old Donald Lee Baker of Rockvale Avenue, Azusa, had set out that morning on a bicycle ride with his new friend, eleven-year-old Brenda Howell, who was visiting a married sister. The children were told that the bike ride was to be a brief one, for Helen Baker, Donald's mother, wanted him to be home by 8:30 a.m. so that he might accompany her to church services.

When Donald and Brenda had not returned by evening, Mrs Baker and her husband Jesse, a chemical plant foreman, picked up Brenda's sister, Mrs Mary Edwards, and the three of them notified the police.

Officers soon located Brenda's bicycle and Donald's jacket in the brush near the reservoir at the edge of the Angeles National Forest. Navy divers were commissioned to search the mile-long, sixty-foot-deep body of water, while police officers, sheriff's deputies, and hundreds of volunteers began carefully to scour the area.

No trace of the two children was ever found.

On 23 March 1957 eight-year-old Tommy Bowman stepped around a corner of a forest trail just ahead of six members of his family and vanished without a trace. This particular forest trail happened to be in the same Devil's

Gate Reservoir area above the city of Altadena, not far from Azusa in California's Angeles National Forest, where Donald Lee Baker and Brenda Howell had disappeared on 6 August 1956.

Within hours after the distraught Bowman family had notified the authorities of Tommy's disappearance, the area was being searched by over four hundred volunteers, trained rescue dogs, mounted patrols, and bush beaters. Woodsmen thoroughly examined any crevices into which the child might have crawled or fallen. The forest trail on which Tommy was last seen was crossed and recrossed by dozens of keen-eyed outdoorsmen. The extensive search was supplemented by low-flying helicopters that crisscrossed the entire area again and again.

To those experts knowledgeable in the ways of woodlore it was obvious that Tommy had not slipped off the trail. No dislodged rocks, torn-away shrubs, or broken branches betrayed such an accident at the spot where Tommy had last been seen.

And it must be remembered that the boy's family claimed to have been only a few steps behind him. They would surely have heard Tommy cry out if he had somehow tripped and fallen off the forest path or if he had been snatched by someone. Even if the boy had been unable to scream or shout, the family would have been close enough behind him to have seen him fall or be grabbed by a molester.

Volunteers and professionals searched for little Tommy Bowman for a week, but it appeared that the boy had been literally plucked from the earth by some unseen and unknown force.

July 13 1960 marked the day of six-year-old Bruce Kremen's first YMCA hike. It also marked the day that the boy would disappear without a trace and become an addition to the list of the unfortunate who were being claimed by California's Forest of Disappearing Children.

Little Bruce had been brimming with enthusiasm for the hike at the outset of the adventure, but the altitude seemed to be too much for him. Noticing the boy's discomfort, the group leader told Bruce to return to the main camp and to rest. The leader said that since the troop was still within sight of the camp, it would be best if the boy went back at once.

The conscientious leader halted the column of eager junior woodsmen while he walked with Bruce until they were within just a few yards of the camp's perimeter. Sending the boy on with a wave and a smile, the leader turned to rejoin the troop of laughing, jostling boys.

Although it was just a few yards to the camp, little Bruce Kremen never made those last few steps. For some terrible, inexplicable reason, he vanished without a trace just nine days before his seventh birthday.

More than three hundred volunteers continued to comb every foot of the forest within ten square miles for twelve days before they regretfully called a halt to their futile search. Bruce Kremen had become another tiny victim of whatever demon inhabited the Devil's Gate region of the 690,000 acres of wilderness.

In each of four mysterious disappearances in that four-year period, the exhaustive efforts of hundreds of experienced volunteer and professional searchers produced not a single scrap of clothing, not a solitary identifying possession, not a corpse, a skeleton, or even a skeletal fragment. The authorities were forced to discard every possible lead. Sex maniacs, kidnappers, wild animals, freak accidents – all were eliminated as a result of meticulous investigation.

In such weird crimes as the above – in which one is certain that a kidnapping and/or homicide has taken place but is left with no corpse to prove such a grisly event – one begins to wonder if it might not be possible, as in the Arnold Schwarzenegger film *Predator*, that there are extraterrestrial or multidimensional entities that intrude into our world just as our sportsmen embark on seasonal safaris to Africa or Alaska. If such a science fiction scenario – frightening as it may seem – could possibly have any basis in reality, then we would certainly be able to sympathize with the stalwart Los Angeles police officers in *Predator II*, who discover that our entire planet appears to be a vast game preserve for some intergalactic hunter.

Such a cosmic crime would truly rank among the weirdest – and deadliest – of all!

CHAPTER NINE

MANSLAUGHTER

MERCY KILLER TAKES LIFE OF AILING UNCLE, THEN DISCOVERS HE DID NOT HAVE FATAL ILLNESS

In January 1990, loving niece Leesa Duval tearfully declared her love and devotion to her sick uncle, then pumped six bullets into his brain. The act was intended to be a mercy killing for Alex Cortellis to allow him to escape the cancer that he believed was ravaging his body.

However, after his death, an autopsy conducted by the police revealed that Cortellis had suffered only from an easily controlled diabetes. A simple visit to a doctor and he could have led a normal life. What is more, he would not have been murdered – and he would not have forced his beloved niece to become a murderer.

In point of actual fact, Leesa Duval and Alex Cortellis were not actually related, but Cortellis, a jeweller in Toronto, Ontario, Canada, had been close family friends with her parents for so many years that everyone, including Cortellis, referred to her as his niece.

When Cortellis became ill, he shunned medical doctors. Later, when he began to lose weight at a rapid rate and developed open sores on his feet, he was certain that he was dying of cancer.

When he had shrunk to a mere 100 lbs and resembled a living skeleton, he called Leesa to his bedside.

Cortellis begged her to perform an act of mercy and put him out of his misery. She could use the gun that he had bought for protection.

At last persuaded to commit the deed because of her deep love for the man, Leesa swore an oath of secrecy to Cortellis – but she felt that she had to confide in Heidi, the woman with whom her 'uncle' had lived for twenty years.

Then, on that fateful night in January, with tears streaming down her face, Leesa shouted her love for Alex Cortellis and emptied the revolver into his skull at point-blank range.

Once the deed was accomplished, she walked into the living room to join Heidi and to wait for the ambulance and the police to arrive.

Although Leesa Duval was charged with first-degree murder, a jury found her guilty of murder in the second degree. If her attorney is persistent, he may get her a suspended sentence because of the very strange extenuating circumstances.

As a Toronto police detective observed as he assessed the irony of the so-called 'mercy killing', the tragedy would never have occurred if Alex Cortellis had made one simple visit to a medical doctor.

SUSPICIOUS WIFE TRACKING UNFAITHFUL HUSBAND IS KILLED WHEN SHE TRIES TO BREAK INTO THE WRONG HOUSE

Ellen Hunt of San Antonio, Texas, was convinced that her husband, Sam, was having an affair. One Sunday in November of 1990, she persuaded a friend to ride along with her while she tracked him down and caught him in the act with another woman.

Ellen had a pretty good idea where Sam might be, and as she drove down a street looking for his car in a particular driveway, she suddenly spotted a grey Sentra and was certain that it was her husband's. Too angry or too excited to check the licence plate, Ellen told her friend that she was going to crash the party.

Determined to break up what she believed to be Sam's rendezvous with another woman, Ellen began to force her way into the house. But just as she lunged through the door, a man with a revolver fired at her.

Ellen Hunt's friend ran down the street screaming for help. As she fled in horror, she could not help noticing another grey Sentra parked in a driveway a few doors down from the house in which Ellen had been shot. She went to that house and found Sam Hunt inside.

Ellen Hunt was pronounced dead at the hospital. The homeowner who shot her was questioned and released.

VIOLENCE BEGETS VIOLENCE! STRAY BULLET KILLS GUNMAN WHO SHOT PRIEST

The Lord does work in mysterious ways.

Late on Good Friday evening in April 1990, Father Henry Murray of Queens, New York, was mugged as he walked to his church. When Father Murray resisted the attack by Cliff Flynn and Barry Cole, Flynn shot him in the right arm. The slug passed through his arm and penetrated his right knee.

Fortunately for the wounded priest, a watchman making his night rounds heard the sound of gunfire and turned his flashlight on the muggers. Rather than risking a firefight with the watchman, the two young men fled into the darkness.

Father Murray was taken to surgery, then admitted, a few days later, to a medical centre to undergo a programme of physical therapy for his injured leg.

At noon, eight days later, Flynn, who had successfully evaded the police investigation, was standing on a street corner when an angry dispute erupted somewhere behind him. He paid little heed to the familiar street sounds of cursing and threats. They had nothing to do with him.

Flynn was about to continue on his way when gunshots caused him to spin around to check out the hassle. One of the young men involved in the quarrel had pulled out a pistol and was firing at the other youth, who was wildly attempting to dodge the slugs. Flynn, in this case an innocent bystander, caught a stray bullet in the heart and fell dead in the street.

Not long after Father Murray had crumpled on the street on Good Friday evening, Barry Cole, the youth who had participated in the mugging, decided that it was time to visit relatives in Pittsburgh. He wanted nothing to do with the shooting of a priest. Flynn was too quick on the trigger for him.

Perhaps it was his conscience that was troubling him on that April evening at around 8:30 p.m. when he sat on board a subway train with his uncle, for suddenly he blurted out that his friend Cliff Flynn had shot a man in Queens.

While his uncle expressed his horror and concern, Cole went on to tell him that he had just learned that that very day, only six hours before, Flynn had been shot and killed on a street in Queens.

Amazingly, Cole participated in bringing about retribution for his own part in the mugging, for he was completely unaware that the two men seated near him were plainclothes transit police officers. With quiet efficiency, they arrested him as soon as he and his uncle stepped off the subway train.

Cole was charged with attempted robbery, assault, and weapons charges. The youth whose bullet brought down Cliff Flynn was charged with second degree murder.

A spokesperson of the New York City Police Department represented all those who believe in divine retribution when he declared that as far as he was concerned, 'God took a hand in bringing Flynn and Cole to justice.'

CHAPTER TEN

MASS MURDER

THE ENIGMA OF CHARLES MANSON AND HIS GRISLY FAMILY: WHY DID THEY KILL SHARON TATE AND HER FRIENDS?

Today, watching film clips of Charles Manson in prison, it is difficult to imagine how the wild-eyed, dishevelled little man could have been capable of casting a spell that would bend young men and women to his murderous will. As weird as it might seem today, the ravings of this silly, illiterate, hostile malcontent set in motion one of the most brutal crimes of the century.

Early in the morning of 9 August 1969 members of the 'Manson Family' committed the sadistic murders of actress Sharon Tate, her friends Jay Sebring, Abigail Folger, Voityck Frokowsky, and a young innocent bystander, Steven Parent. The 'Tate Murders' cast unprecedented fear upon the Hollywood motion picture community: if the loonies could get to Sharon Tate, they could get to any other actor who might have become a symbol to the crazies of God-knew-what.

Manson, who was called 'Satan', 'God', or 'Sweet Daddy-O' by his young female disciples, had been in jail for most of his life.

His unwed mother was a teenaged hustler who picked up trucks in cheap roadhouses and bars. Shortly after his birth on 11 November 1934 in Cincinnati, Charlie was sent to his grandmother's home in McMechen, West Virginia. Later, the child lived with a quarrelsome uncle and aunt.

Neighbours recalled Charlie as 'a poor little kid' who never received any love or affection'.

When he was eight years old, Charlie joined his mother as she drank in bars and hustled men. The two of them lived in run-down apartments on the ugly side of the city.

By 1945, his mother had found a travelling salesman who promised a steady relationship, and she took him along with her to Indianapolis. However, her lover did not consider young Charlie a part of the deal, so she tried to place him in a foster home.

Later, the state authorities made him a ward of the county. He was sent to the Gibault School for Boys, a custodial institution for homeless or wayward boys. Charlie escaped after ten months.

Manson remembered that he kept running, and they kept putting him in tougher reform schools. He ended up in the reform school at Plainfield, Indiana – the toughest of the state. By his own testimony, he escaped from there 'twenty-seven or twenty-eight times'.

Manson was thirty-five years old when he was indicted for the Tate murders. Brown-haired, brown-eyed, and slender, he had spent twenty-two years of his life in state or federal prisons. Uneducated, untrained, and barely able to read, the only things that he had learned in his years of confinement were how to steal cars, how to pass bad cheques, and how to pimp.

On those rare occasions when he was out of prison and free on parole, Manson exhibited an obsession with sex. He lived with one woman, then another, in a free and easy life that held no lasting responsibilities.

In the early 1960s, Charles Manson stole and cashed two US Treasury cheques. He was promptly apprehended and sent to the federal prison at McNeil Island, Washington.

According to one of his former followers, it was here that Charlie began to explore offbeat philosophies and the occult. Manson also liked to play his guitar, and he learned that he could influence his cellmates with music. He worked hard, attempting to train his voice, and he began to write his own songs.

When Charlie walked out of prison in March 1967, a whole new world had been created while he was behind bars. The flower children had launched the hippie movement, and the Haight-Ashbury section of San Francisco had become their golden gloryland. Charlie got himself a hillside pad there and started to collect his followers.

One of his first disciples was an attractive, long-haired, nineteen-year-old brunette named Patricia Krenwinkel. A 1966 graduate of Los Angeles High, she was considered a reserved, conservative young woman by all who knew her. But when she met Charles Manson, she was transformed instantly into a cult camp follower.

Patricia Krenwinkel fell under Manson's mystical spell so quickly that she abandoned her automobile in a parking lot and left without picking up her paycheque. A few weeks later, her family received a brief letter informing them that she was going off to 'find' herself.

A number of young women were drawn to the mystical minstrel by some weird power. A few young men also joined his cult, and the group became known as the 'Charles Manson Family'.

Charlie was a magical man to those desperate, seeking young people who came to sit at his feet. 'There was so much happiness around him' remembered one of his former cult members. 'Charlie knew the answers to everything. If you had a problem, he could always come up with the answer.'

Manson led his cult in weird chants. He adopted mystical rites from other traditions and shaped them to his own unique personality. He began to make prophecies. Anyone who doubted or questioned his godlike stature was threatened with expulsion from the group.

In May 1968, with the hippie scene fading out in San Francisco, Manson and his subservient clan headed south toward Los Angeles. Led by their mystical guru, the flock of young people converted an old schoolbus into a rolling pad and headed for the City of Angels. The bearded, long-haired Manson planned to make a fortune as a songwriter and a musician in the movie capital.

Manson and his nomads met and moved in with thirty-four-year-old Gary Hinman, a musician. The Hinman home was labelled the 'pig farm', a refuge for weirdos.

A year later, Hinman was murdered by Manson's followers when he tried to toss the Family out of his home. The killing of Gary Hinman is believed to be the first murder perpetrated by Manson and his cultists. The musician was discovered slashed to death in his home. The bloody legend 'political piggy' was scrawled on the walls of the death house.

Then came the terrible night of carnage in the Tate-Polanski mansion.

Susan Denise Atkins, one of Charlie's girls, told of a half hour of unbelievable butchery: 'Charlie told us to hit that particular house. He gave his instructions to me, Tex [Charles Watson], Linda Kasabian, and Pat Krenwinkel. We were to use a black '58 or '59 Chevy. We had two changes of clothes. One was our creepy crawlies – black costumes to wear when we 'creepie-crawled' around people's houses.'

Atkins also stated that Manson did not give his orders directly to the women, but spoke through Tex Watson, a member of the Family. The girls were ordered by their satanic leader to do whatever Watson commanded.

Armed with knives, a change of clothes, and a gun, Tex Watson drove the girls toward the Tate mansion. Susan Atkins remembered Watson explaining to them that the house had once belonged to Terry Melcher, Doris Day's son. Although Melcher no longer lived there, their mission was supposed to be part of a plan to frighten him for having failed Manson in some undetermined way.

When they pulled up in front of the mansion, each of the girls was armed with a knife. Watson parked the vehicle, snipped the telephone wires, then led the Family members on a terrible orgy of murder.

The Family members were surprised when Steven Parent walked down the driveway from the caretaker's cottage. Watson rushed to the young man's automobile, fired twice, and killed him.

The assassins next moved towards the mansion. Watson forced open a window, crawled inside, and opened the door for his companions.

Voityck Frokowsky, a friend of Sharon Tate's husband, director Roman Polanski, was asleep on a couch in the living room. Awakened by the intruders, he stared in drugged disbelief at their bizarre outfits and demanded to know who they were.

One of the girls told him that they wanted money.

Frokowsky said that he would give them all the money he had. He fumbled for his wallet, couldn't find it, then remembered that it was on the desk.

Watson pulled out his pistol. 'Don't move,' he commanded. 'Don't move or you're dead. I'm the devil, and we're here to do my business.'

The disturbance alarmed Sharon Tate and the other guests, Abigail Folger and Jay Sebring, who were brought into the living room. The very pregnant Tate was wearing a short, see-through nightgown with a halter beneath it. She wanted to know what the intruders were going to do with them.

Watson did not hesitate to pronounce their deadly mission: 'You're all going to be killed!'

Sebring, a celebrated Hollywood hairstylist and a former lover of Tate's, studied the five armed strangers. Perhaps his practised eye could determine that they were on drugs, for he made the decision to fight for his life. He was shot, stabbed, and collapsed dead in the living room.

Although Frokowsky had been bound on the couch, he managed to break the nylon cords that tied him. One of the girls stabbed him again and again as he raced out of the house, screaming for help.

Watson pursued the wounded man, clubbed him with the pistol, then shot him in the back.

Abigail Folger, heiress to the Folger coffee fortune, was stabbed as she tried to run towards the caretaker's house on the southern edge of the grounds. She was slashed to death on the lawn.

Sharon Tate battled two of the girls, but was overpowered and forced back on a couch. 'All I want to do is to have my baby,' she pleaded.

'Kill her!' the girls chanted. They continued to stab and to slash at her body even after she lay dead on the floor.

Someone in the Family dipped a towel in the blood that flowed from Tate's breasts, and a red-stained *PIG* was painted on the mansion door.

On the night following the Tate murders, Patricia Krenwinkel recalled that she and Leslie Van Houten were tripping out on LSD. Then, along with Linda Kasabian and Tex Watson, they went for a drive and ended up in front of the home of Leno and Rosemary LaBianca, wealthy Los Angeles business owners.

The couple was grabbed by the Family and tied up. Rosemary LaBianca was stabbed to death as she lay on her bed.

Patricia Krenwinkel dimly recalls seeing a man [Leno LaBianca] on the floor. 'I remember thinking, "You won't be sending your son to war." And I guess I carved "WAR" on his chest. I picked up a big fork and plunged it into his stomach.'

Throughout the lengthy ordeals of their arraignment and trials, Manson's female disciples insisted that their guru was innocent of any blame in the gruesome slayings. Life in Manson's nomadic Family was described as an ideal existence. Manson himself was declared to be living 'perfection' and the 'best lover ever'.

According to most professional analysts of the enigma that is Charles Manson, he was not a mystic or a guru. Rather, he was an extroverted, glib, extremely persuasive person who ruled his Family with supreme tyranny. If he liked something, so must everyone in the group. If he directed his hostility towards an object or a person, the others were expected to develop their hatred. If he declared that sleeping in the nude was right, then everyone must do it. When he decided something was wrong, then that practice was forbidden.

Manson preached that if everyone could drop their sexual hangups, then all of their problems would be solved. He initiated the new female members of the commune, and they spent their first day in the Family making love to him. If a new girl refused to engage in oral-genital sex, she was expelled. Manson claimed that oral sex was an important indicator that the girl had been liberated from her middle-class sexual inhibitions.

In Manson's cosmology, he and all of humanity were God and Satan at the same time. He also professed that every human was part of all others, which, in his philosophy, meant that individual human life was of no consequence. If you killed a person, you were just killing a part of yourself, so that made everything all right.

The mystery of Charles Manson is that somehow, in the manner of a ritualistic magician, certain of his motions, movements, and gestures could give him such power over other people that they would wantonly kill other human beings without a trace of guilt permeating their consciousness. The fear that Manson inspires is that somewhere another self-styled guru of death sits chanting his mystical melody of murder to another group of enchanted disciples.

THE QUIET GENTLEMAN WHO KILLED THIRTEEN IN TWELVE MINUTES

Howard Unruh had been considered a gentleman throughout his adult life. Friends and acquaintances believed him to be one of the most mild-mannered young men that they had ever met. Unruh seemed to be the kind of man who would go out of his way to avoid trouble. His fellow employees, his former Army buddies, the members of his church congregation all confirmed his quiet and responsible nature.

Yet on 6 September 1949 the twenty-eight-year-old ex-GI descended the steps of his mother's apartment, walked out on the streets of Camden, New Jersey, and started to kill people in what seemed to be an indiscriminate pattern of murder.

No one who knew Howard could understand what had made him go off the deep end. But later the police investigation revealed that the black day had been festering in the young man's mind for a long time.

Although it is impossible to state exactly when Howard began heading for that day of violence, certain factors of his personality had remained constant throughout his entire life. A better than average student, Howard Unruh had favoured more scholarly activities, but he seemed to have been well accepted in spite of the fact that he did not participate in athletics.

His parents were middle-class working people, and even though they had separated during Howard's adolescence, their marital situation did not change his life significantly. Although he lived with his mother, he remained on good terms with his father. His only brother was married and lived in the suburbs.

Howard's academic plans to become a pharmacist were interrupted by World War II. To the surprise of all those who knew him, the quiet lad from Camden made a good soldier, a very efficient fighting man.

In fact, Howard Unruh's superiors rated him top notch. During training, he had been ranked as a sharpshooter, and his accuracy did not diminish under combat pressure.

As a gunner assigned to a tank command, Unruh participated in the Battle of the Bulge. Earlier, he had taken part in the bloody trek up the length of the Italian peninsula.

Howard was also accepted by his fellow GIs, even though they gave him a hard time about his refusal to drink or go out with girls. He preferred to remain by himself and read his Bible.

But military life and the war did have an effect on the quiet man. One of Howard's buddies, who later became a New York police officer, recalled glancing at a page of his diary and being astonished to find that Unruh had written with delight of the German soldiers he had killed. After the terrible mass murder in Camden, the officer revealed that it had been his suspicion that Howard Unruh had had the soul of a murderer all along and that the Army had simply channelled that killer instinct for the duration of the war.

As a civilian, Unruh continued to be fascinated by firearms, and he began collecting pistols. He set up a firing range in the basement of his apartment, and he spent hours there, improving his already superior marksmanship.

Out of the service, he renewed his interest in pharmacy. He was consistently at the top of the class in the college preparatory courses that he took, but when he enrolled at Temple University in Philadelphia, he had somehow lost most of his ambition.

He told his mother that he was suddenly finding it difficult to readjust to civilian life. He seemed unable to concentrate in class.

Although he complained that life was beginning to lose meaning for him, Unruh and his mother continued to attend a nearby church, and he also participated in a Bible class. The only girlfriend he was ever known to have had was a member of the church.

Howard's benign appearance masked an inner turmoil that was about to erupt in twelve minutes of violent death for his neighbours. He had begun to view the world around him as an alien place, its inhabitants as his enemies. His new mindset was the result of many years of mounting suspicion, which his twisted personality had transformed into a violent hatred of his fellow humans. Howard Unruh had become what psychiatrists term a paranoid schizophrenic.

Early in the summer of 1949, Howard ceased to attend church, and at the same time, he stopped dating the girl that he had been seeing. He was undergoing some radical adjustments in his life, and he had begun to seek sexual gratification from other men. It was a crucial time in his paranoia. He felt as if the entire world were peering at him.

It was a part of Howard's normal pattern to leave his mother's apartment by the rear door and cut through the backyard of the next-door neighbours, the Cohens. Mr Cohen was the owner of the drugstore that adjoined the flat where he, his wife, son, and mother lived. On this particular day, the elderly woman shouted in irritation from behind her screened window, 'Hey, you! Do you have to go through the yard?'

Howard was not hurt by the old lady's complaint, but by the fact that she had not called him by name. Back in his room, he added the incident to a long list of grievances that he had already recorded against the Cohens – which included their 'sin' of slamming their screen door late one night.

The Cohens were not the only people against whom he intended retaliation. Howard had complaints recorded against nearly all of his neighbours. Each of these 'violations' would have been considered insignificant by a normal person, but to Howard, they had acquired tremendous significance. Each notation recorded in his book marked an individual for killing.

On 5 September 1949 Howard sublimated his anger for one more day by installing a gate in the fence that enclosed their small yard. The gate would allow him to get in and out of the yard without crossing anyone else's property, and it would prevent the prying eyes of neighbours from falling on him.

That night, Howard went out, and when he returned about 3:00 a.m. he was astonished and enraged to find that the new gate had disappeared.

As always, his calm demeanour prevailed, but the incident became the proverbial back-breaking straw. Although it would later be learned that pranksters had taken the gate away, Howard was positive that his cruel and accursed neighbours were to blame. He had no proof and no way of determining exactly who had taken the gate, so he would just have to kill everybody.

The following morning, his mother made eggs and cereal for his breakfast. Mrs Unruh was so disturbed by the wild look in her son's eyes that she ran from the house. Nearly hysterical, she took refuge in a friend's house, and there she fainted when she began to tell of the hatred that she had glimpsed in Howard's angry expression.

Howard was a little upset by his mother's reaction. It threw his schedule off and forced him to start earlier than he had planned. Also, he had intended to kill his mother first to spare her the humiliation of his acts.

He went to his room, loaded a Luger pistol and another handgun, and put a knife in his coat pocket. All the extra clips for the Luger were loaded also, and he shoved them into the other pocket of his coat. He picked up a tear-gas cartridge before he left the room, then walked outside and vaulted the fence instead of walking through the gateless hole in it. He made his way over a neighbouring yard, then through an alley that brought him to the side-walk on River Road, between a cleaning establishment and a shoe repair shop.

The time was 9:20 a.m. Howard Unruh was about to begin one of the deadliest walks in the annals of crime.

His first stop was the shoe repair shop.

Cobbler John Pilarchik looked up from his work as Unruh entered the store, and he was met by the barrel of the Luger. Howard's expression never changed as he squeezed off two quick shots. The blasts echoed through the little shop, and Pilarchik pitched headlong on the floor.

When Unruh left the cobblers shop, he turned left, heading for the corner of the block and the Cohen drugstore. But before he got there, he stopped at the barber shop owned and operated by Clark Hoover.

When Unruh entered, the barber was busy giving six-year-old Orris Smith a preschool haircut. Orris's mother, Mrs Edward Smith, was standing next to the boy, who had mounted the plastic horse on which the barber trimmed the hair of young would-be cowboys. Mrs Smith's eleven-year-old daughter and two boys from the neighbourhood were also in the barber shop.

The expression on Unruh's face was one of extreme impatience. He had come after the barber, Clark Hoover, and the Smith boy was in the way.

He shot the boy in the head, then levelled the pistol at Hoover, shooting him once in the body and once in the head.

Unruh paid no attention to the other people in the barber shop. Mrs Smith snatched up her son's body, and together with her daughter and the neighbourhood boys, ran out of the place.

It was only a short walk for Unruh to reach the corner of Thirty-second Street and River Road and the entrance to the drugstore. He was about to enter the pharmacy when the Unruhs' insurance agent, James Hutton, stepped in front of him.

Howard had no quarrel with Hutton, so he asked him politely to step aside. Hutton stood stock still, frozen, astonished at the sight of the Luger in Unruh's hand.

Because the man was in his way, Howard fired the pistol twice more – one slug in Hutton's body, the other in his head. The insurance agent fell dead to the sidewalk.

Having disposed of the temporary obstacle in his path, Unruh entered the drugstore to seek out the chief targets that he wanted most of all to place in front of his Luger. But Cohen had seen what had happened at the entrance of his store, and he had run upstairs to warn his family.

MASS MURDER

When the gunman could not find anyone in the store, he, too, walked slowly up the stairs.

Mrs Cohen had hidden her son in one bedroom closet, while she herself had squeezed into the other. Unruh entered the bedroom and seemed to sense someone in the bedroom closet. He shot through the closet door, then opened it and watched the woman's body crumple to the floor. He shot her again, this time in the head, apparently unaware of the footsteps of the escaping boy.

In the next room, Unruh found the druggist's mother on the phone, trying to call the police. The Luger banged twice more, and the woman dropped the phone as she fell dead.

While the killer had been occupied with shooting the woman, the druggist and his son had climbed out a window and on to the sloping roof of the building. Unruh picked off Cohen with a shot in the back. The druggist's body fell to the sidewalk.

Unruh wanted to take no chance that the man might survive. Taking careful aim, he shot through the window again. The bullet entered the man's skull and ended his life. Of the four people who had been in the building when Unruh entered, only one remained alive.

But the gunman was far from finished. There were other neighbours who had to be repaid for the insults and slights that Howard imagined they had inflicted upon him. He began to retrace his path, his stride slow and deliberate.

A car had stopped on River Road to investigate the sprawled form of James Hutton, and a man knelt on the sidewalk beside the body of the lifeless insurance agent. Without hesitation – and again with deadly accuracy – Unruh levelled the Luger and fired. Motorist Alvin Day, in an effort to aid a man beyond help, had forfeited his life.

With practised smoothness, Howard slammed another clip in the Luger, then walked across the street to where a car waited for the lights to change. He shot the woman driver in the head through an open window, then poked the barrel of the pistol inside the car and blasted away until the woman's ten-year-old son and aged mother were also dead.

The tall, taciturn murderer walked on as if nothing extraordinary had occurred, then fired two shots in the locked door of a bar-restaurant before recrossing the street on a diagonal that brought him back to the shoe repair shop where the carnage had begun.

Down River Road, a truck driver was climbing down from his cab. It was a long shot, but Unruh proved his marksmanship once again when he hit the driver in the leg.

On the other side of the cobbler's shop was Tom Fegrino's tailoring business. Unruh entered the store and proceeded to the back room where he found Fegrino's terrified wife. Her pleas had absolutely no effect on the gunman as he impassively triggered the two shots that snuffed out her life.

Outside again, Unruh chanced to see a movement in a nearby window. Most of the residents had sought cover by now, but three-year-old Tommy Hamilton had wandered to a window and was looking curiously through it when the glass shattered in front of him. The boy fell to the floor, dead.

Unruh left River Road by way of an alley running between the tailor's and the cobbler's. He walked to a house that opened to Thirty-second Street, and entered it.

Mrs Madeline Harrie was home with her two sons, Leroy, fourteen, and Armond, sixteen. Although her first thought was to flee, Mrs Harrie decided that she would not be driven from her home. Her older son rushed Unruh; and perhaps because of the body leaping at him, Howard's aim was inaccurate for the first time. His two shots only wounded Mrs Harrie and Armond. He would have fired again, but, mercifully, he had run out of bullets.

Howard Unruh trotted lightly back toward the apartment where he lived, vaulted the fence, and ran inside. Behind him he could hear the thin wail of police sirens. He had barely climbed the stairs when the first police car arrived at the intersection.

The time was 9:32 a.m. Only twelve minutes had passed since life on the street had been interrupted in its normal routine. Soon the entire area swarmed with law-enforcement officials.

At the office of the Camden *Courier-Post*, city editor Phillip Buxton had a hunch that he felt compelled to follow. He had heard the killer's identification reported over the police radio and quickly snatched up the telephone book to look for the name. When he had located the only possibility, he dialled the number, hoping that the deranged mass murderer would answer the phone.

Barricaded in his apartment, Unruh still acted unconcerned. Even while the bullets of the police tore through the plaster walls, he calmly answered the phone. The story of this incredible telephone interview was carried on the front page of the *Courier-Post* and adds elements of the bizarre and ironic to an already weird and sick account.

'Is this Howard?' journalist Buxton asked.

'Yes, this is Howard,' the killer answered with his usual courtesy. 'What is the last name of the party you want?'

'Unruh.'

'Who are you and what do you want?'

Buxton said that he was a friend who wanted to know what 'they' were doing to him.

'Well, they haven't done anything to me, yet,' Unruh replied, 'but I'm doing plenty to them.'

Buxton wanted to know how many Howard had killed.

'I don't know yet – I haven't counted 'em; but it looks like a pretty good score.'

'Why are you killing people?'

Howard answered that he didn't know, but he was too busy to talk any more. He would have to talk later.

Unruh was indeed very busy. The police had begun blasting tear gas through the shattered windows, and, almost immediately, the killer lost interest in returning their small-arms fire. He could have chosen to retaliate with the tear gas that he also carried; but instead, he decided to give himself up.

Fifty police guns were trained on Howard Unruh as he walked out of the back door with his hands in the air. He was frisked and handcuffed immediately.

'What's the matter with you?' someone from the crowd demanded as the police led Unruh away. 'You a psycho?'

'I'm no psycho,' Unruh replied calmly. 'I have a good mind.'

Howard Unruh was never brought to trial. A team of over twenty specialists was unanimous in their assessment that he was insane. Not many people wanted the polite, quiet murderer on the loose, however, and he was placed in the New Jersey State Mental Hospital at Trenton.

During one interrogation he told psychiatrists, 'I'd have killed a thousand if I'd had bullets enough.'

Fortunately, Howard Unruh had run out of ammunition.

THE BIBLE STUDENT WHO BELIEVED HIS 'HOLY MISSION' WAS TO STRANGLE LANDLADIES

Earle Nelson had always had unusually large hands. When he was a pious young boy, he claimed that God had given him such big hands so that he could better hold the Bible. Even as a youngster, Earle had been a serious student of scripture, but tragically, after the unfortunate lad spent six weeks in the hospital following a trolley car accident, the words of Holy Writ began to take on a new meaning.

His aunt, who cared for the orphaned boy, offered prayers of thanks for the miracle of her nephew's recovery, but she had no gift of divination that would permit her to perceive the twisted thing that had begun to grow in the dark recesses of the boy's mind.

Nor could she hear the voices that summoned Earle to withdraw in moody silence to his room to memorize the Bible passages that referred to harlots and whores. He had become obsessed with 'Jezebels', 'Delilahs', and the 'Whore of Babylon'.

Earle Nelson celebrated his twenty-first birthday by luring a neighbourhood girl down into the cellar of her home, where he tried to rape her. The girl's screams brought her father, but it took the additional restraining arms of two patrolmen to subdue the powerful and determined young man.

Young Earle was convicted of attempted rape and sentenced to the state penal farm for two years. In less than a week, he broke free, but he was soon recaptured.

Six months later, he escaped again. This time he was apprehended on a stormy night as he stood leering through the bedroom window at his cousin Rachael as she undressed for bed.

The authorities transferred Earle to the state penitentiary. Three months later, on 4 December 1918, while working in the prison laundry, Earle picked the lock and somehow managed to crawl over a twenty-foot wall without being seen by prison guards.

It would be nine years before he would be behind bars again – nine years and twenty murdered and sexually violated women.

On 12 August 1919, under the assumed name of Roger Wilson, he married a lovely young schoolteacher. 'Roger' would embarrass his wife in public places by loudly accusing her of flirting with other men. When she attempted to placate him. Earle would call her a 'silly whore, a strumpet of Babylon, a harlot'. Then he would be on his knees before her, begging forgiveness in his loudest voice.

Although he had restrained the perverse demons within him for quite some time, Earle finally lost control and beat his wife savagely. When she was able to stagger to a doctor, she was taken immediately to a hospital.

Earle came to visit his wife, but while he was in the hospital, he began to force himself upon her while she lay in her bed. When her moans of pain at last brought a doctor to her rescue, Earle went nearly berserk at the man's interference with the fulfilment of his sexual pleasure. He accused his semi-conscious wife of having an affair with the doctor, and screaming his outrage at everyone in sight, he walked out of the hospital and out of the life of the frightened woman who had married him. She would not know until eight years later just how fortunate she was to have survived her life with 'Roger Wilson'.

On 20 February 1926, Earle followed Mrs Clara Newman up three flights of stairs as the San Francisco landlady showed the new boarder to his room. When they reached the room on the top floor, he could do nothing other than obey the demon voices' command to kill.

Afterward he stared at his hands. The Lord had given him big, powerful hands, but it was the demon voices that had given him an awesome sense of power.

On 2 March, Mrs Laura Beale was found strangled and raped in her rooming house in San Jose. Journalists were quick to point out the similarities between the two murders, and they began to issue printed warnings to the effect that a maniac was stalking landladies.

On 10 June, the ravished body of Mrs St Mary was discovered beneath the bed of an unoccupied room in her boarding house.

A Santa Barbara landlady fell victim to the monster's insatiable appetite for murder and perverted sex on 26 June.

On 16 August, a landlady in Oakland was attacked with such appalling violence that even seasoned police officers blanched at the sight.

The month of September was quiet. Then, on 19 and 20 October in Portland, Oregon, the vicious strangler claimed two victims in two days.

By November, ten landladies had been murdered and

violated, and the authorities still possessed not a single lead to the identity of the man who hunted landladies.

Then, early in December, his voices told him to leave the West Coast and travel to the Midwest.

On 23 December, he murdered Mrs John Berard of Council Bluffs, Iowa. On 28 December, in Kansas City, Missouri, he raped and strangled both a landlady and her eight-month-old daughter.

By spring, Nelson had moved farther east, and on 27 April 1927 he strangled Mary McConnell of Philadelphia. Jennie Randolph of Buffalo, New York, fell victim to his awful hands on 30 May.

On 1 June, Earle bloodied Detroit with the murders of Minnie May and Mrs M. C. Atworthy. As far as could be determined, this was the only instance in which he killed two adult women on the same day.

Mrs Mary Sietsome of Chicago became his eighteenth victim on 3 June. With the exception of the infant daughter of Germania Harpin, all of Earle Nelson's victims had been landladies. It was tragically ironic that the strangler sought his 'whores of Babylon' among landladies, all of whom had been hard-working married women and mothers.

At this point the inner voices told Earle to leave the United States and to head north for Canada. In Winnipeg on 8 June, he rented a third-storey room in the home of Mrs August Hill.

On the very night that 'Mr Wilson' moved into Mrs Hill's rooming house, a pretty young girl named Lola Cowan, who supported her family by selling artificial flowers, disappeared. Inexplicably, Earle had altered his *modus operandi*. For some reason never to be understood, the voices had spared Mrs Hill and directed their murderous fury toward a teenaged girl.

A few nights later, William Patterson returned home from work to find the naked and ravished body of his wife shoved roughly underneath their bed. Her death seemed to fit the descriptions of the series of murders in the United

States, yet the pattern had been altered: Mrs Patterson was not a landlady.

Police officers began making routine checks of all recent arrivals to their city. When they called upon Mrs Hill's rooming house and were shown the room of 'Roger Wilson', they found the three-day-old corpse of Lola Cowan under his bed.

Two days later, Constables Grey and Sewell, working out of Killarney, just twelve miles north of the international border, stopped a man walking on the highway who identified himself as Roger Wilson. They handcuffed the suspect, took away his shoes, and locked him in an interrogation room while they went to make a telephone call to Chief of Detectives Smith in Winnipeg.

When they returned fifteen minutes later, they found to their horror that the man who was quite likely the murderer of twenty women had escaped. He had picked the lock on the handcuffs and the door and walked out of the station house.

The entire female population of Killarney was locked up under armed guard in the town hall, and a five-hundred-man posse spread out to search for the killer – while Earle Nelson slept peacefully in a barn just a block away from the room where he had escaped the constables.

The next morning, Earle calmly boarded a train out of town. He probably would have made good his escape if he had not got on the very train that was bringing Chief of Detectives Smith and several police officers to Killarney to assist in the search. Earle was recognized, apprehended, and brought to trial for the murder of Emily Patterson in Winnipeg.

No one heard Earle utter a single word throughout the entire course of his trial. Rather, he seemed to be listening to sounds and to voices that remained unheard by jury, judge, attorneys, and courtroom spectators.

Interestingly, the voices remained with Earle only until he was judged guilty and sentenced to be executed. From that moment until his last, he was left to pace his cell and wonder about the voices that had commanded him to kill.

On 12 January 1928 Earle Nelson quietly ascended the thirteen steps of the gallows. Before the hangman dropped the black hood over his head, Earle declared that he stood innocent before God and man. And, from his warped perspective, he forgave all those who had wronged him.

'BORN TO RAISE HELL' – HE COMMITTED ONE OF THE MOST BRUTAL CRIMES OF THE CENTURY

On 11 September 1990 Illinois prison officials at Stateville Correctional Center near Joliet denied parole for the seventh time to Richard Speck, a convicted murderer who has spent half of his life behind bars for the brutal slaying of eight student nurses in July of 1966. The Illinois Prisoner Review Board stated that the forty-eight-year-old killer would continue to serve his sentence of up to twelve hundred years.

When Chicago Coroner Andrew Tolman had completed his unenviable task of examining the eight cruelly stabbed and strangled young nurses, he declared that in his six years as a coroner and in his many years as a police surgeon he had never seen any crime or atrocity so bad. 'This is the crime of the century,' he told reporters.

Dr Edward Keller, head of Chicago's Psychiatric Institute, was prompted to state: '[The murderer] was a sexual psychopath, a deep-down woman hater who was completely gratified by what he did.'

On that terrible after-midnight carnage on 14 July 1966 there had been nine nurses who had been marked for death by Richard Speck. Miraculously, one of them escaped and lived to narrate for the world the awful ordeal of the monstrous hours of horror in which her friends died one by one.

The nurses had all been students at the South Chicago Community Hospital. Three were graduate nurses from the Philippines. The other six were Americans. Eight of the young women lived in a townhouse on the south side of Chicago in a pleasant neighbourhood known as Jeffrey Manor. Everyone who knew them regarded them as quiet, serious, well-mannered 'good people'.

Earlier on the evening of Wednesday, 13 July, Philippine exchange nurse Luisa Silverio had stopped by the dormitory and had been invited to stay for dinner by Valentina Paison and Corazon Amurao, both twenty-three years old, also Philippine nurses. As a special treat, Valentina had prepared a special Philippine dish, and they urged Luisa to join them.

On any other night, Luisa Silverio later told reporters, she would have quickly accepted the invitation of her friends. But on this particular night, there was something strange and foreboding about the house that had bothered her. 'It seemed so queer, so dark. It was as if nobody was inside.'

Luisa Silverio made her awkward apologies, then returned to her own dormitory – and to life.

When Richard Speck broke into the kitchen around midnight, he had to pass a bulletin board where a note issued the admonition: 'Students are not to allow anyone into the townhouse without the housemother being there.'

The deadly intruder crept upstairs to the front bedroom where Corazon Amurao was sleeping. There was a knock at her door, and when she opened it, there was a man standing there.

Corazon noticed the strong odour of alcohol before she saw the gun in his hand. He forced her down the hallway as he awakened the other women and herded them into one bedroom. In a soft, quiet voice he kept telling them that he would not hurt them. He just needed some money to go to New Orleans.

Speck used a knife to cut bedsheets so that he could bind the nurses. He continued to speak to the women in a soft voice, and as he bound and gagged each of them, he asked her where she kept her money. When the woman had either obtained the cash she had on hand or indicated where it could be found, Speck would truss her up and make her lie down on the floor.

Outside the townhouse, Suzanne Farris, twenty-one, was riding around in the car of her future sister-in-law, Mary Ann Jordan, twenty, a fellow student nurse. They had been discussing plans for the forthcoming wedding of Suzanne and Mary Ann's brother, and they had lost track of time. They dropped student nurse Pat McCarthy, another friend, off at her dormitory, then Suzanne invited Mary Ann to sneak into her townhouse to spend the night. For one thing, Suzanne said, Mary Ann lived at home, a long-distance drive at that late hour – and besides, if she spent the night, they could chat more about the wedding.

At 12:25, the two nurses met another resident of the dormitory, twenty-two-year-old Gloria Jean Davy, who was also rushing toward the entrance of the townhouse at 2319 East 100th Street. The three of them giggled about their just missing the 12:30 curfew, then they stepped inside – and closed the door to safety behind them.

'There was some light outcries by the girls who came in late, but it wasn't much,' Corazon Amurao remembered.

Once Speck had collected their available cash, he bound and gagged the three latecomers and made them lie down on the floor with the six other young women. For a time, he sat on the floor in the midst of the nurses, saying nothing, only fingering the knife that he had used to prepare their bonds.

'Then he took one of the girls out of the room,' Corazon said. 'After a few minutes, he came back alone and took another of the girls.'

It was obvious to Corazon what was on the mind of the tall, blond man with the soft voice. She and Merlita Gargulla, twenty-two, set about attempting to loosen their bonds.

Corazon whispered to the others that once she got free, she would untie them. Then she would pick up a steel bunk ladder and hit the intruder over the head with it. The seven of them could easily overpower him if they all jumped him at once.

'Lie still, Cora,' one of the American nurses told her. 'He's told us that he meant us no harm. Let's not start anything that will make him do anything crazy.'

The other two Philippine nurses agreed with Corazon. If the intruder was so harmless, why hadn't the other two women been returned to the room? In harsh whispers they begged the Americans to free themselves and to jump the man. Why lie there helplessly until he decided what he wanted to do to them?

'But maybe if *we* are quiet and calm, *he* will remain quiet and calm,' one of the American nurses argued.

When she saw that it was useless to debate the matter, Corazon Amurao rolled under one of the bunk beds and hid. There she cringed and prayed while the tall, blond intruder took the girls one by one out of the room.

Later, she remembered, none of them uttered more than 'a little scream'.

In the frenzy of the horrible acts that he was perpetrating, Richard Speck either lost track of the number of his victims or else he had known before his invasion of the townhouse that the dormitory housed eight girls. If such were the case, he was unaware that there were nine nurses present that night, since Suzanne Farris had invited Mary Ann Jordan to stay the night.

At 5:00 a.m., Corazon Amurao heard an alarm clock go off. Summoning her courage, she crept out from under the bed, crawled on to a balcony ledge, and began to shout hysterically: 'All my friends are dead! Oh, God! I am the only one alive!'

A neighbour ran into the centre of the street and flagged down a squad car driven by Patrolman Daniel Kelly. He knew many of the nurses inside. He had dated the sister of Gloria Davy.

Kelly and Officer Leonard Ponne, who had been called by another neighbour, entered the townhouse through the back door that Speck had left unlocked.

'Bodies were strewn all over the place,' Patrolman Kelly was later to tell journalists. 'There was blood everywhere. It was something that cannot be described in words.'

On the couch in the downstairs living room, they found the naked and lifeless body of one of the nurses. She had been strangled and mutilated.

In the middle bedroom, the blood from three bodies had drenched nightgowns. In the other bedroom were the corpses of three more young women.

One of the young women found in a bathroom had been stabbed nine times and strangled.

Despite his own shock, Patrolman Kelly managed to calm Corazon Amurao and to obtain a description of the killer from her.

Homicide Commander Francis Flanagan lived in Jeffrey Manor and had been able to walk to the scene of the murders in about five minutes. A veteran of three thousand homicide investigations, the detective was appalled at the savagery with which the nurses had been slain.

Commander Flanagan thought it likely that the murderer was a seaman, because of his repeated statement to the victims that he needed to get to New Orleans and because of the expert square knots with which the nurses' hands had been tied. Flanagan also agreed with other detectives, who felt that the man was an ex-convict or someone with a police record who was fleeing from the authorities. New Orleans had long been acknowledged as an ideal port from which an itinerant seaman on the lam might ship out.

Another piece of the bloody puzzle that made the seaman thesis quite tenable was the fact that the hiring hall of the seaman's union was less than half a block away from the scene of the murders. A visit to the hall resulted in a photograph of Richard F. Speck, a man who matched Corazon Amurao's description of the murderer. Speck was a seaman who just missed sailing on an ore boat that had left Indiana Harbor on 11 July.

While Ms Amurao was going through a stack of 180 mug shots of men in their twenties who had a record of crimes against women, an investigating officer slipped a copy of the photograph of Speck that he had obtained from the seaman's union hiring hall.

She had been flipping through the mug shots, discarding one after another. Finally she hesitated. 'This one is similar,' she said, tapping a fingernail on the photo of Speck. 'Everything except the hair. In the picture ... he wears it long. That night it was shorter.'

In the mean time, on North Clark Street, a team of detectives was following Speck's trail through a string of seedy bars in the company of local prostitutes.

On the morning after the murders had occurred, Speck was nearly thrown out of a bar for horsing around with a knife. The bartender had grown surly when Speck insisted on demonstrating both to willing and unwilling patrons how best to kill someone with a knife. 'This knife has killed several persons,' he boasted.

When a television news report of the discovery of the mass slaying of the young nurses came on in the beer joint, Speck was heard to state soberly that 'it must have been a maniac that done it'.

At 12:30 Sunday morning, 17 July 1966, Dr LeRoy Smith, resident surgeon on trauma duty at Chicago's Cook County Hospital, made a hasty appraisal of the bloodied derelict who had just been brought in from a skid-row flophouse on West Madison Street. The semi-conscious man was bleeding from a cut under the left elbow, plus a cut vein and a superficial slash on the bony portion of the right wrist. *Instant diagnosis*: A botched suicide.

Dr Smith's eyes narrowed thoughtfully. There was something about the man, something familiar. The doctor's attention became fixed upon the patient's blood- and filth-encrusted upper left arm. He dipped a cotton swab in some alcohol and began to dab away at the gore and grime until he uncovered the motto that had been needled into the man's flesh: 'Born to Raise Hell.'

Dr Smith slowly unfolded the newspaper and studied the photograph of the man the police suspected of murdering the eight young nurses. 'What is your name?' he asked the patient as he prepared him to receive a transfusion.

'Richard Speck,' the man answered in a weak whisper. 'Do you collect the $10,000 reward, Doc?'

Dr Smith was too stunned by the man's response to reply to the question. The search was over. The man who had committed the 'crime of the century' was lying at his mercy.

'Kathy,' the doctor called softly to the attending nurse. 'This is the man the police are looking for. Please get hold of them right now.'

During the trial and after Richard Speck's subsequent imprisonment, a great deal of research and investigation was made into the killer's past. It has been suggested that he may have committed many other stranglings and stabbings of women.

One witness recalled seeing Speck in a Dallas bar just a little less than a year before the gory murders of the Chicago nurses.

'He was standing there at the bar, reading a newspaper,' the witness remembered. 'When he happened to find the name of a friend who had been arrested for some minor infraction of the law Speck snorted in disgust. "One of these days," he says, "it won't just be a little item about me in the newspapers. It'll be the whole front page!"'

In those words of terrible prophecy, Richard Speck foretold his place on the front pages of the newspapers of the world as the perpetrator of one of the most brutal mass murders in the annals of crime.

CHAPTER ELEVEN

MATRICIDE

HE KILLED HIS MOTHER BECAUSE SHE DATED TOO MUCH

Although it would seem like the most perverse kind of reasoning to nearly anyone who would listen to Gabriel Petra's anguished cries, the twenty-year-old swore that he loved his mother so much that he was forced to shove a kitchen knife in her throat.

Parlour psychiatrists will always come up with worn-out theories about Oedipus complexes when a young man seems jealous of his mother's affections, but maybe that's judging the situation too much from the head and not from the heart.

Everyone could see that forty-year-old Monica Petra was beautiful. Her large brown eyes combined the seemingly disparate energies of childlike innocence and smouldering passion. Long dark hair tumbled around features that somehow seemed totally unscathed by the swinging lifestyle that this woman of Naples enjoyed. And all of her friends knew that Monica had a taste for nonstop parties and handsome men.

Divorced not long after Gabriel's birth in 1970, Monica, in pursuit of *la dolce vita*, had subjected the child to a seemingly endless parade of sweethearts and lovers. All his life, Gabriel had felt as though he had been shunted aside so that his mother could pay more attention to her paramours.

According to a family friend, there had been steadily

mounting tension between mother and son because of her love life. When Gabriel learned that the businessman with whom she was having her current affair was barely older than himself, it seemed to be the last straw. Gabriel moved out of the house, and as an act born of the twin frustrations of anger and despair, he began to do drugs.

At the time of the murder, Gabriel had taken an apartment near the home of his mother and her young boyfriend. Gabriel would start an argument every time he visited Monica, loudly declaring his loathing of her current relationship.

Then, one awful night in July of 1990, Gabriel grabbed a kitchen knife and plunged it again and again into his mother's throat. His fury continued unabated until she lay dead at his feet.

Just a few hours later, he turned himself in to the police and freely confessed to the crime of matricide.

'I killed my mother because I adored her,' he stated during his lengthy confession to the Naples, Italy, police. 'I left her in a sea of blood because I loved her. But she didn't have time for me. She never had time for me. She thought only of her boyfriends. She ignored me. She always made me feel so alone.'

BOY SHOOTS MUM WITH HUNTING RIFLE WHEN SHE REFUSES HIM A COCA-COLA

On 14 November 1990 in Lille, a northern French city near the Belgian border, police reported that a six-year-old boy shot and seriously wounded his mother with a hunting rifle when she refused to allow him to drink a Coca-Cola.

Angered by his mother's firm denial of his pleading for a Coke, the boy (whose anonymity was protected by the authorities) left the kitchen of their apartment and walked to his parents' bedroom where he knew a hunting rifle was kept in a closet. He removed the weapon from its hiding place, checked the breech and found it to be empty. The boy was able to load the rifle himself, and he walked back to his mother and shot her in the abdomen.

It may have been the rifle's eardrum-splitting report or the sight of his mother falling bleeding to the floor that finally snapped the six-year-old gunman into the realization that he was not playing cops-and-robbers with his friends. Somehow he was at last made to understand that he had just fired a real gun at his real mother and he had seriously harmed her.

After he pulled the trigger and reality rushed in upon him, the boy ran downstairs to seek help from neighbours. His mother was taken to a hospital in Lille, while he was placed in the temporary custody of a children's home.

CHAPTER TWELVE

MOBSTERS

JOHN DILLINGER'S $200,000 FIVE-HUNDRED-YARD RUN

It was on 20 April 1934 that the strangers stepped into Emil Wanetka's Little Bohemia roadhouse eight miles south-east of Mercer, Wisconsin. The smiling bartender had hoped that he was about to entertain a carload of generous tourists from the big city, but his anticipation quickly evaporated when he recognized the faces before him.

Right there in his roadhouse stood the most notorious gang in the Midwest – the kill-crazy, carve-them-up mobsters of John Dillinger – and the boss himself.

'We just want to relax and enjoy ourselves,' Dillinger informed Wanetka in a soft voice. The mobster's tone implied that if Wanetka just pretended that they were ordinary tourists and minded his own business, he just might get out alive.

The bartender recognized the men backing the slight form of Dillinger from the pictures of his gang that appeared regularly in the newspapers. There was the surly Van Meter, the murderous Baby Face Nelson, together with gunmen Tommy Carroll and Pat Reilly.

Wanetka needed no time at all to reach a mental decision not to buck that crowd. The mob and their giggling, gum-smacking play-girls could raise all the hell that they wanted to – and he would just keep right on smiling and pouring drinks.

For the next seventy-two hours, the mob gave vent to all

sorts of tensions. They swilled beer from Wanetka's cooler and punched the cash register to get coins for the jukebox.

Dillinger and his gang needed a little relaxation. They had fled Chicago with G-men hot on their trail. While the mob headed for Wisconsin, Dillinger's moll and gangland courier, Patricia Charrington, took a million dollars' worth of bonds and securities to Minneapolis to be converted by a fence into $200,000 in cash. She had then delivered a suitcase packed with the loot to Dillinger and had returned to the Windy City to find a new hideout on Chicago's west side. All the gang had to do now was to stall for time.

Time was one precious commodity that would soon be in short supply for the Dillinger gang. Federal agents had received a tip that the mob was hiding out in the Wisconsin woods, and they had managed to trace them to the little tavern outside of Mercer. Even as Baby Face Nelson dropped another nickel in the jukebox, G-men were surrounding the Little Bohemia.

The government men had spotted the armed guard on the roof of the tavern and were proceeding with extreme caution. None of them was rash enough to underestimate Dillinger's skill with a sub-machine-gun. A quick council was called, and the agents decided to wait until after dark to make their move.

Then, just as the Federal agents were about to close their net on the Dillinger mob, Fate intervened in a most bizarre manner. Three men walked out of the Little Bohemia and got into a car. Although these men – John Hoffman, Eugene Boisoneau, and John Morris – were not associated with the Dillinger gang in any way, the word was quickly whispered around the cordon of G-men that three members of the mob were making a break.

An agent ordered Hoffman to stop his car. The startled man blinked his surprise at the armed figure that had suddenly materialized at the side of the road, and he decided that he would keep right on driving.

The failure to comply with the command was all that the circle of agents needed to open fire on the three men.

Boisoneau was killed; Morris was seriously injured; and Hoffman, miraculously untouched by the rapid gunfire, jumped out of the car and ran for the tall timber.

Inside the tavern, the burst of gunfire tipped the mob to the Federal agents' presence even more completely than if the G-men had thrown a rock through the window wrapped in a note that announced their invasion plans.

Dillinger grabbed the suitcase with the cash, ordered his men to slip out through a back window and meet at another roadhouse down the highway. At their boss's command, each of the thugs ran in a different direction to further confuse the pursuing FBI agents, who were now beginning their siege on the Little Bohemia.

It did not take long for the agents to comment on the noticeable lack of returning gunfire from the roadhouse. When they forced the door, they found Emil Wanetka and the mob's three party girls cowering behind the bar.

The Dillinger mob met at the appointed roadhouse, stole a car, and headed back to Chicago. The sharp-eyed mobsters immediately noticed that their boss no longer carried the suitcase with the $200,000, but no one dared to bring the matter up for discussion.

Once they reached the city, Patricia Charrington earned Dillinger's blessings for having found a retreat that would keep the mob out of G-man surveillance. When he was alone with his moll, he told her the details of how they had given the Feds the slip and where he had cached the suitcase full of cash.

According to the gunman, he had run five hundred yards straight north of the Little Bohemia where, in the centre of a semicircle formed by three trees, he had dug a hole in the ground and buried the suitcase. He promised her that as soon as the heat was off, the two of them would return to Wisconsin to reclaim the loot.

It was a promise that Dillinger would be unable to keep. A short time later, G-men shot the gangster down outside the Biograph Theatre in Chicago.

Patricia Charrington went to prison, and when she was

released, she never again expressed any interest in recovering the buried suitcase with the $200,000 swag. She did, however, give explicit details to a lawyer.

The lawyer soon discovered, as have so many subsequent seekers of Dillinger's unclaimed take, that the mobster's directions were probably not all that accurate. He had told his moll that he had run 'five hundred yards straight north' of the Little Bohemia. First of all, let us remember that Dillinger made his dash after dark. It would be extremely difficult for any man to pace off the yards while running in the dark – especially one who had to fear that bullets would soon be whizzing by his ears. Secondly, it is almost impossible to run for five hundred yards in a straight line in any direction in the dense Wisconsin woods.

The most vital fact of this aspect of weird crime, however, remains unassailable: Dillinger did bury $200,000 somewhere in the woods eight miles south-west of Mercer, Wisconsin, and it has never been recovered.

THE MYSTERY OF BIG JIM'S LOST GEMS

Before the underworld of Chicago had ever heard of Al Capone or Frank Nitti, Big Jim Colosimo, who made most of his money from the sweat off the backs of his pleasure girls, ruled the gangland scene.

Big Jim had a thing about diamonds. He bought them from jewellery stores or private dealers, and on occasion, he would relieve a jewel thief of his take at the point of a snub-nosed .38.

Big Jim wore loud, flashy suits and complemented his well-manicured nails by wearing a diamond ring on each finger. The studs on his shirt front were all of diamonds, and he sported a huge, diamond-encrusted horseshoe on his suspenders.

As the ultimate expression of his penchant for the precious gem, the big hoodlum carried pockets full of diamonds wherever he went. Whenever Big Jim was under any amount of tension, his nervous fingers would seek the sanctuary of a pocket filled with diamonds. He was like 'Captain Queeg' in the *Caine Mutiny*, only Big Jim rolled diamonds, rather than steel balls, between his fingers to soothe his anxieties.

When Big Jim was killed by a power-hungry rival in the winter of 1920, the total value of the gem-loving hoodlum's estate was calculated to be a mere $40,000. According to underworld experts, this was about one-twentieth of what the gangster overlord was worth.

Immediately the Chicago crime scene began to be obsessed with the mystery: what had happened to all of Big Jim's gems?

Some of Big Jim's hoods claimed that their late boss had liquidated the precious stones and had spent the loot on a woman. But the woman in question, Dale Winter, emphatically denied the hypothesis. According to her, Big Jim was a tight man with his bank roll.

Other mobsters, who considered themselves to be confidants of the gang boss, said that Colosimo had hidden the diamonds – about $800,000 worth – in downstate Illinois. To date, such a cache, if it ever existed, has never been found.

Cronies began reconstructing the last days of the Chicago baron's life and came to the conclusion that he had buried his treasure trove somewhere just outside of Crown Point, Indiana.

But why had the diamond-loving thug committed his precious stones to the soil? This is the way the story seems to shape up:

Big Jim had entered into a loveless marriage of convenience with a girl from a 'good family' around the turn of the century. Early in 1920, the jaded overlord met Dale Winter, an actress-singer, and he convinced himself that at last he had met the woman who could supply him with the romance that he felt his life was lacking. He phoned his lawyers and instructed them to arrange a divorce with his wife.

Mrs Colosimo settled for a flat $50,000 and received the total sum without a whimper of protest from the smitten hoodlum. Three weeks after the divorce became final, the mobster was married to Dale Winter at Crown Point, Indiana.

When Big Jim returned from the honeymoon, his friends were astonished to see that his diamond accoutrements had disappeared from his suits. The suits themselves were of more sophisticated cut and obviously reflected the taste of his new wife.

If Big Jim himself had changed, so had the framework of his organization – undoubtedly without his awareness.

During the weeks that he had been pursuing his infatuation with Dale Winter, he had turned much of his gang's administrative work over to his right-hand henchman, Johnny Torrio. Torrio had come up through the ranks of Colosimo's combine and he was assured that he now knew enough about the business to take over the reins of the organization from the boss – especially now that the old man had gone soft over a dame.

A week after Big Jim had returned from his honeymoon, he was shot down in one of his own restaurants while conferring with his organization's secretary, Frank Camilla. There was nothing to connect Torrio with the assassination, but no one needed to be officially notified that the ambitious hood had accomplished his power play.

When the auditing of Colosimo's estate had been completed, Torrio, as principal heir, was less than ecstatic about the paltry sum of money to be divided with the grieving singer in her black widow's weeds.

'A lousy forty grand!' he snarled at his henchmen. 'What happened to all of Big Jim's diamonds?'

Everyone in Chicago had known about the big thug's obsession with the glittering stones. Either his young wife had killed that obsession or else she had supplanted it with another interest.

Colosimo's attorneys wrote the diamonds off as a permanent loss. One lawyer ventured a theory that Colosimo, having been liberated of his lust for power and of the desire to ostentatiously display his wealth, had buried the precious gems as a kind of gesture of his independence from their former mesmeric spell.

A gang member, who claimed to be 'like that' with Big Jim, recalled that Colosimo had said basically the same thing – without the intellectual symbolism.

'I got the dame now,' he had told his crony. 'I don't need the rocks any more. I got 'em buried outside of Crown Point, though, and they'll always be there if I need them. But as long as I've got Dale, I ain't got no use for 'em.'

If you should consider setting out with spade in hand for Crown Point, please accept this word of caution: even today, a favourite summer diversion among a certain group of Chicago hoodlums consists of an expedition to Crown Point to 'hunt for Big Jim's gems'. The serious purpose of these forays soon degenerates into an excuse for outdoor drinking parties and hell-raising brawls, but nevertheless it would not be a good idea to run afoul of the syndicate's safari.

THE MATRIARCH OF MURDER AND MAYHEM WHO BECAME THE CRIME WORLD'S BLOODIEST MAMA

At dawn on 16 January 1935 special agents of the FBI began moving through the mists hanging over Lake Weir, Florida, to surround the cottage in which Ma Barker and her son Fred were holed up.

'Kate Barker,' shouted the leader of the picked group of agents, 'your cottage is surrounded by the FBI. We want you and your son to come out one at a time with your hands up!'

There was no response from the cabin. Several more commands were issued by the FBI leader without receiving any reply from the notorious mother-and-son terror team. At last the agent issued an ultimatum and stated that they would drive them out with tear gas.

Five minutes went by.

'Come out at once or we'll open fire on the cottage.'

After another five minutes had agonizingly ticked by, Ma Barker shouted her defiant answer: 'All right, go ahead!'

The matriarch of murder and mayhem was not about to go down without a fight. She appeared briefly at the window, her machine-gun held expertly in her thin arms. With her jaw jutting in bulldog determination, Kate Barker strafed the trees and undergrowth with a vicious spurt of machine-gun fire.

The battle lasted for hours. FBI agents lobbed tear-gas bombs into the cottage and concentrated heavy fire from automatic weapons on the firing points within.

Surrender was simply not in the tough woman's vocabulary. And her son Fred, like his three brothers, always did just exactly what Ma told him to do – even if the order was to fight to the death.

When the agents were at last able to enter the cottage, they found Kate Barker dead, a single bullet in her heart, still clutching a machine-gun in her left hand. Fred was doubled over, already stiffening in death, a .45 automatic at his lifeless fingertips. He had sustained eleven bullet wounds.

The Barkers had collected enough firearms in the cottage to equip a regiment. There were, along with more mundane pieces, two Thompson sub-machine-guns, a Browning twelve-gauge shot-gun, two .45 automatics, two Winchester rifles – plus machine-gun drums, automatic pistol clips, and enough ammunition for the heaviest siege.

'Well,' sighed an agent as he surveyed the carnage before

him, 'we finally got the mother hen. Now how long will it take before we can get the rest of the brood?'

Of all the gangs of the Thirties, the Barker-Karpis combo had the worst reputation. Ma Barker and her four sons teamed with Alvin Karpis and his shot-gun sadists, and the awful allies specialized in banks, blood, and butchery. An extremely effective band of plunderers, the Barker-Karpis mob listed mail robberies, prison breaks, assorted holdups, and kidnappings in their repertoire of evil.

J. Edgar Hoover once pointed out that the FBI had apprehended many men and women who had killed often and inhumanely, yet they still possessed a side to their nature that was not wholly despicable. But of the Barker gang, the top G-man was moved to write:

'Without a single exception, Ma Barker, her four sons, and the mobsters they commanded, were monsters, and pity was a word of which they had never heard. They moved in a welter of blood, mail robberies, bank holdups, kidnapping, and pitched machine-gun battles. They loved nothing better than to kill a police officer, and if some innocent bystander fell to the same hail of bullets that did not matter either. They executed their own traitors, bought corrupt police officials, fixed paroles and prison breaks. Their anarchy fouled the very roots of law and order.'

Born eighteen miles north-west of Springfield, Missouri, in 1872, Arizona Donnie Clark grew up in the wild, mountainous Ozarks. When she married George Barker, she became a malicious mother hen who carefully instructed her four male chicks in the finer points of ruthless criminal activity.

'There's only one sure way of doing business with a banker,' Ma told them. 'And that's with a machine-gun!'

Herman, Lloyd, Fred, and Arthur made apt and attentive pupils.

'Maybe some of them fancy educated fellers can out-talk poor folks like us,' she admitted, 'but if you just pull that little trigger and make some noise – why, it's as good as a college diploma!'

Of Scots, Irish, and Indian ancestry, Arizona Donnie, nicknamed 'Kate', grew up in the stark reality of extreme poverty among the inhabitants of the Ozarks. Although she had no one to tutor her in the nefarious skills of crime, she possessed a remarkably intuitive grasp of the steps required to become a big-time criminal. Her ruthless nature was a great asset, as was her natural resourcefulness and extreme sense of independence.

From their earliest childhood, she indulged her sons and encouraged them to be crafty and cruel. George 'Pa' Barker almost immediately surrendered all responsibility for rearing their sons to his wife – but the boys knew that they had a strong father figure in their hard-as-nails mother. Pa Barker was soon eased out of the picture – perhaps mercifully so.

Fred Barker – Ma's favourite – met Alvin Karpis in 1930 while they were both doing time in the Kansas State Penitentiary. Karpis had been dubbed 'Old Creepy' by his fellow inmates because of the cold, fishy stare that he would transfix on anyone who was foolish enough to cross him.

Karpis had just the sort of con man's mind that appealed to Fred, and the prison cell comrades quickly formed a business relationship when they left the grey walls.

The two hoodlums thought so much alike that Sheriff C. R. Kelly of West Plains, Missouri, didn't have a chance when he approached their automobile on a routine check. He was cut down with machine-gun fire before he could unholster his own weapon.

The murder of the sheriff put the heat on the Barker-Karpis gang, and in 1932, Ma and the boys fled to St Paul, Minnesota, with her lover of the moment, Arthur Dunlop. The stopover in St Paul was a brief one, for Ma's intuition told her that the police were about to close in on them.

J. Edgar Hoover, director of the FBI, often remarked how uncanny it was that the Barker-Karpis gang, 'throughout its lifetime', was able to 'smell' danger before it was too late for them.

But Ma Barker left the police with a gory souvenir of her visit. It seems that she suspected her lover of having squealed to the police. The terrified Dunlop had protested his innocence, but Ma had already made up her mind.

'How else did the cops know about our hideout in St Paul?' the queen of crime demanded.

Although there was no evidence to indicate Dunlop's betrayal, Ma, for some inexplicable reason, had already decided that her lover had tipped off the police as to the gang's whereabouts. Now, as always, she was about to administer her own particular brand of justice.

Dunlop flicked frightened eyes from his paramour to the tough mobsters who flanked her on either side. They were far out in the country, on the shore of a lake near Webster, Wisconsin.

Ma commanded Dunlop to strip, to take off all the fancy clothes that she had bought him. Then as he stood before her stark naked, she ordered her boys to hold him tight.

While the condemned man protested his innocence in blood-curdling screams of pain, Ma Barker snapped open a switchblade knife and carved the mark of the squealer into his cheeks.

The naked, bullet-battered body of the mutilated Dunlop was found by fishermen. Near his mangled corpse lay a woman's blood-stained glove.

Ma always seemed to enjoy playing the role of judge and jury to those whom she felt had transgressed the laws of her criminal society. In Tulsa, Oklahoma, she decreed the death of J. Earl Smith, a criminal lawyer, who had unsuccessfully defended mob member Harry Bailey for his participation in a bank robbery. Although the evidence was overwhelmingly against Bailey, Ma hissed into a telephone: 'You shouldn't have lost, counsellor!'

Smith's riddled body was found on the golf course of the

Indian Hills Country Club, fourteen miles north of Tulsa.

A vicious and successful raid on the Cloud County Bank at Concordia, Kansas, netted the Barker-Karpis gang over $240,000. Ma used some of the loot to grease palms and to buy a parole for one of the Barker Boys from the Oklahoma State Penitentiary. Incredibly, she also bought a two years' 'leave of absence' for another mobster from penitentiary officials.

Reinforced by the men they had 'paroled' from prison, the gang moved to Minneapolis, and in December 1932 took the Third North-western Bank. While in the process of the heist, the gang chopped down two policemen and a citizen whom Ma suspected of memorizing their licence plates.

Tired of knocking over banks, Ma suggested a try at kidnapping. Their first victim was William A. Hamm, Jr., of the Hamm Brewing Company of St Paul, whom they grabbed on 14 June 1933. Gratified with the $100,000 ransom, the matriarch with a machine-gun decided that the systematic snatching of members of wealthy families was a much easier way to make quick money than the risky robbing of banks. She decreed to her brood that rather than plundering the Commercial State Bank in St Paul, they would, instead, kidnap its president, Edward George Bremer, and this time they would stick a $200,000 ransom price on their prey.

The first attempt to grab Bremer in the spring of 1934 resulted in failure for the gang and in bloodshed for two innocent men. Two pilots from North-western Airways, wearing their commercial uniforms, pulled up behind the kidnappers and were mistaken for police officers. They were cut down by the mob's machine-guns.

Ma was not deterred in the least by their error in judgement, and the determined Mother Superior of the mobsters made new plans to snatch Bremer as he dropped his daughter off at school. This time the gang was successful, and long and intricate negotiations between the anguished family and the Barker-Karpis body snatchers took almost a month.

The FBI could do nothing but stand by helplessly as long as the tough old gangland matriarch held Bremer in her hideout. At last the payment was made in five- and ten-dollar bills, and the thugs pushed the bank president out of a car on a side road north of Rochester, Minnesota.

It is known that after Ma had obtained the ransom money from the Bremer family, she intended to relay $100,000 of the loot to Havana, Cuba, and exchange it for gold. She was much too cunning not to realize that the Feds had recorded the serial numbers of the bills. It would take time to send the money to Cuba along the intricate gangland route, but it would be well worth it in terms of self-protection.

And now here is another mystery for our annals of weird crime: no one knows what happened to that major hunk of loot.

According to those who rode south in the car with Ma from Rochester, the gangland matriarch stopped the automobile near Chatfield, Minnesota, and, with the help of Fred Barker, carefully buried the money in a strongbox wrapped in a heavy tarpaulin. Fred is said to have complained about the cold and later said that they had uprooted a fencepost while burying the swag.

The plan, of course, was to return to retrieve the treasure as soon as possible, but things just didn't work out that way. The G-men would catch up with Karpis and company in Kansas, and Ma and her son Fred would fight to the death in their cottage in Florida.

Somewhere under one of the fenceposts in the twenty-mile string between Rochester and Chatfield, Minnesota, there could be a mighty rich farmer – if only he knew where to dig!

Although things were going well for the gang after the successful kidnappings in St Paul, Ma thought her men needed another example to quell any thoughts of mutiny before they might occur. Mob member Fred Goetz had committed some minor infraction of the queen mother's criminal code, so he had his face removed with two blasts of a shot-gun.

Such a demonstration proved to be a very effective and dramatic object lesson for the gang. It was so effective that one of Goetz's molls had to be placed in an insane asylum. She had become deranged after witnessing Ma blow away her lover's face, and she cracked under the stress of possibly offending the mighty Ma.

Ever cautious, the matriarch next decreed that her sons should have their faces 'lifted' by Chicago physician Joseph Moran.

'It's for your own good,' she admonished her boys as they underwent the agony of Moran's scalpel. 'Doc will fix it so the cops won't be able to recognize you. And when he finishes carving up your faces, I'll have him scrape away your fingerprints.'

When the physician had completed his handiwork, Ma was disappointed. His best had not been good enough for her. His weighted body was soon sinking to the depths of Lake Michigan.

Moran really hadn't been too skilful. FBI agents had little difficulty recognizing one of the beautiful Barker boys, and they nailed him when he was shacked up with a girlfriend in Chicago. It was in his apartment that they found a map of Florida with a circle around Ocala and Lake Weir.

A quick check brought the FBI information that had filtered up from the natives of the area. They claimed that there was a woman and her son hiding out in a cottage in an area of the swamp frequented by an ancient alligator named 'Old Joe'. It seemed that the old swamp king had resented the invasion of his privacy, and he had alerted the permanent inhabitants of the area with his loud grunts of complaint.

Ma Barker never had an opportunity to administer her

cruel justice to this thick-skinned 'squealer'. True to her code, though, she died with a smoking machine-gun grasped in her practised hands.

In May 1936, about a year and a half later, Alvin Karpis had his opportunity to 'take care of that sissy J. Edgar' when the top Federal agent himself led the raiding party that nabbed the mob in New Orleans. Karpis failed in his boast to take out the head of the FBI.

Six days later, the rest of the gang was apprehended in Toledo, Ohio. All of Ma Barker's bloody brood had at last been put behind bars – or planted under the sod.

CHAPTER THIRTEEN

POISONING

THE VOODOO WOMAN'S COMPLAINT: 'EVERYONE I LOVE SEEMS TO DIE!'

When World War II veteran Dick Luther died of a mysterious malady in January 1950, a large crowd of mourners came to the funeral in Shreveport, Louisiana. Luther left behind his widow, Lola, and their two children, Cheryl and Kathy.

Lola complained to her friends in her soft Louisiana drawl that Dick's death had left her in 'real poor circumstances'. She had assumed that he had a number of health insurance policies, but their sum total was only $2,800.

Of course, she acknowledged, she would receive about $170 a month from his disability from the Veterans' Administration. 'Every little bit helps when you're a single parent with two young girls,' she sighed.

The buxom, shapely widow was not the type of woman who would mourn or miss her husband for very long. She went to work, saved her money, and opened a restaurant in downtown Shreveport. Located in the heart of the business district, Lola's 'Pink Lady' café became one of the most popular restaurants in the city. Her congenial and open personality brought customers flocking to her place.

She had barely established the Pink Lady when a brawny, six-foot Missourian became a steady diner at the café. Hank Carstairs was a cross-country trucker, and he liked Lola's cooking.

Lola liked Hank, and she allowed as how there were times when she could surely use a strong man around the place. Hank and Lola were married following a whirlwind courtship that only lasted a few weeks.

After they had returned from their honeymoon, the copper-haired redhead began to spend more and more time sitting in front of her black voodoo candles and mumbling a kind of song with peculiar words.

When Hank complained that she spent too much time with her 'mumbo-jumbo', Lola answered sweetly that she was making magic for their love and saying prayers to keep him healthy and strong for ever. Hank could hardly gripe and moan about such fine and noble intentions.

What Hank never saw, however, was the little bottle with the skull and crossbones on it. If the voodoo candles and the curses didn't work, Lola could always bolster her magic with some arsenic.

Three months after he had become a bridegroom, Hank Carstairs fell ill and took to his bed. His husky body had ruptured with running sores, and his hands had to be tied behind his back to prevent him from scratching the painful ruptures raw.

Lola hired a nurse, and the two women fed Hank intravenously. But his condition worsened, and the nurse advised Lola that her husband would die unless he was brought very quickly to a hospital.

Despite hospitalization, Hank died. Lola brought out her black widow's mourning clothes, and once again Shreveport's finest citizens attended a funeral for the husband of the shapely redhead.

The next member to die in Lola's family was the mother of her first husband, Mary Luther, who passed away in September of 1955. About eight months later, Kathy Luther, Lola's beautiful, brown-eyed daughter, died a terrible death in the hospital.

To all her consoling friends, Lola uttered the same mournful dirge: 'There must be some terrible curse that strikes down everyone around me. Everyone I love seems to die. It must be the will of God.'

Law-enforcement officers were also beginning to wonder why everyone Lola loved ended up dead. The authorities ordered an autopsy on Kathy and discovered that arsenic poisoning had been responsible for the child's death.

The pathologist explained how a person could be given arsenic over a long period of time, for the poison works in such a manner that the effects are not quickly recognized. Unlike many poisons, arsenic does not produce an immediate reaction, such as convulsions, in the victim. Unless a doctor has been advised to watch for arsenic poisoning, he would probably be unable to make a correct diagnosis of the cause of death without an adequate laboratory workup. Arsenic is a favourite of murderers because the poison is a great imitator that creates symptoms that closely resemble many common ailments.

With the laboratory report establishing Kathy's death as the result of arsenic poisoning, detectives rushed to Lola's home and began to search the premises. They turned up six bottles of a virulent rat poison in which the main ingredient was arsenic. They also located several empty bottles of the stuff – according to one detective, 'enough to kill fifteen or twenty people'.

Lola was arrested and arraigned for trial on a charge of murder. Her arresting officer was astonished that the woman had not appeared to be perturbed by the charges levelled against her.

Dressed in her traditional black dress, composed and serene, the redhead followed the routine in the courtroom as if someone who was a stranger to her were being tried for the heinous crimes.

However, when each prospective juror was asked: 'Would you sentence a woman to death in the electric chair?' Lola was seen to tighten her fingers around the white-bound copy of the New Testament in her lap.

As the trial progressed, witnesses painted a fiendish picture of the Merry Widow. Besides poisoning her relatives, she had forged a will to collect her mother-in-law's estate. The four deaths had netted the copper-haired poisoner about $50,000. The scandalmongers loved it when the prosecutor explained how Lola had blown every dime of the money on her boyfriends.

'She also bought a new Lincoln and spent her blood money keeping up a social whirl that was beyond her means,' the attorney revealed.

Lola's other obsession had cost her a small fortune. She had purchased every bit of paraphernalia that she could obtain that would assist her with her black magic spells. The prosecutor pointed out that she had paid dearly for the 'blessed' equipment that would enable her to perform voodoo rituals. She had also bought elaborate concoctions that were purported to be voodoo love potions to bring back her erring boyfriends.

Lola did not deny her belief in voodoo and the dark powers. 'I believe in things like black magic and voodoo,' she told a hushed courtroom. 'The investigators made fun of me because I messed around with voodoo candles. I have been burning candles for a long time, because I know they bring luck.

'The candles that I used would burn for seven days before they burned out. I burned a white candle for peace and an orange candle to keep people from becoming angry at me. I used to light red candles to bring love into my life.

'I also visited root doctors,' she continued, 'old herb ladies, spirit advisers, and I never let a day pass that I didn't see a fortune-teller.'

Lola told the courtroom that she never went anywhere without her roots. Why, she informed them, there were roots in her purse on the very day that she was arrested. She possessed certain roots that she would place in her mouth so that when she talked to people, they had to do whatever she wanted them to do.

The buxom murderess testified that a fortune-teller had

predicted that her daughter Kathy would die.

'The fortune-teller predicted this two years before Kathy died,' Lola said with great solemnity. 'I was also told in advance about all of the other deaths in my family.'

Following her testimony, a journalist shook his head in disbelief. 'I have a horrible suspicion that she used the fortune-teller to create a self-fulfilling prophecy. Lola made certain that the predictions of death in her family came true.'

Lola Luther Carstairs waited quietly in the courtroom as the jury of twelve men filed out to decide her fate. It did not take them very long to return with their verdict of 'guilty'. The jurors made no recommendation for mercy, and Lola was sentenced to die in the electric chair.

Ultimately, the copper-haired voodoo poisoner was committed to a state mental hospital under a state law that prohibits the execution of an insane person.

THE BEAUTIFUL BLONDE ANGEL OF DEATH FROM CINCINNATI WHO THREW A FAREWELL PARTY IN HER PRISON DEATH CELL

On a lovely May evening in 1938, twenty crime reporters were invited to the most bizarre party ever held in Cincinnati.

'At first I thought it was a gag,' one newsman said to another. 'Who ever heard of a party being thrown in a death cell two nights before the condemned prisoner's execution?'

His colleague grinned wryly around the stump of a dead cigar as a prison guard escorted them to the cell. 'If anyone could bring it off, you know Anna Marie Hahn could.'

'Hey, here come a couple more,' the shapely blonde in the death cell said, laughing as she spotted the two journalists. Her manner was that of a social register hostess rather

POISONING

than of a woman scheduled to die in the electric chair. 'Glad you two could make it to my "going away" party!'

Anna Marie smiled expansively as she called to another crime reporter, 'Hey Al, what do you think of your "seductive blonde" now? Man, the way you wrote about me, I bet people thought that I was a movie star instead of a murderer!'

The newsman named Al awkwardly returned the condemned woman's smile. 'I really meant all those words, Anna. I think it's a damned waste that you are going to . . .'

Al caught himself, started to apologize, got busy lighting a cigarette. He had almost said the F word – 'fry'.

'Yeah,' Anna said as she sobered. 'In two nights I get the hot squat.' Then, shaking her long blonde hair and rekindling the fire behind her sparkling blue eyes, she grinned and shouted, 'So let's live it up tonight! Hell, the way some of you guys live, I'll probably still outlast some of you.'

The condemned woman's raucous bravado brought a smattering of strained laughter from the journalists gathered in her death cell.

'Now I want all you guys to have a good time,' she continued. 'I talked the warden into letting me throw this party for you because you were all so good to me during the trial. The only thing I ask is that you give me a good writeup when . . . when it's all over.'

Blonde, buxom, beautiful Anna Marie Hahn murdered at least a dozen elderly men by the time she was arrested at the age of thirty-one.

'I was an angel of mercy,' she explained indignantly in the courtroom. 'I dislike seeing old people suffer. All I ever did was to make them comfy.'

The jury decided that Anna Marie was an angel of murder who had managed to write herself into the wills of each of the men she had poisoned.

Anna Marie had emigrated from Germany with her husband and baby son when she was twenty-two. A good wife and mother, she had only one fault – expensive tastes. Her extravagances drove her honest and hard-working husband Philip to distraction with her demands for bigger and better things that only more money could buy. And in America of 1930, money wasn't to be had for a minimum of effort. That is, unless you found a way of securing it that was somewhat less than honest.

Anna Marie instinctively knew what every woman with a beautiful face and a fine figure knows: a pretty woman need never lack for money. And if the pretty woman has very few moral scruples, it is even easier to locate the loot.

The well-endowed blonde began going out nights to the beer garden in the German colony in Cincinnati. Gifted with a pleasant contralto voice, Frau Hahn soon became popular as a singer of folk ballads of the old country.

To the old German gentlemen who tilted their beer steins in nightly bouts of nostalgia, she became the personification of the country that they had left behind. Her blondeness, her bountiful figure, her warmth and charm all totalled up to the perfect prototype of the ideal fräulein, a veritable living *valkyrie*.

As might be expected, some of the elderly men were more panting than paternal in their feelings toward Anna, but she never resisted their advances. She would sit at their tables and sing to them of the old country and never once complain about the hand on her knee. Nor did she protest the presents that they began to shower upon her.

'Where's old Hans tonight?' she asked a group of the man's cronies.

'*Ach*, he so hated to miss out on your singing, but he's not feeling so well tonight.'

'That's too bad,' Anna Marie said, her sigh of disappointment ending in a practised pout. 'Maybe I'll stop in and see him on my way home tonight.'

'*Gott in Himmel!*' shouted one of the elderly gentlemen,

jerking his mouth away from the stem of his pipe. 'Would you stop and see me if I should take ill?'

'Of course I would, Wolfgang,' Anna laughed. 'You are all my sweethearts.'

'If that should truly be the case,' squawked a white-bearded patriarch, 'I'm not going to bother coming to the beer garden any longer. You can come to my home and visit me!'

Although the men might have been joking, Anna Marie Hahn could not have been more serious. She did stop by and visit old Hans that night. And the next night. And it wasn't too long after her last visit that the elderly man died from some sort of intestinal affliction.

'Too bad about old Hans,' they all said at the beer garden. And many of them knew that the wonderful angel of kindness, Anna Marie Hahn, had stopped by his house to minister to him. Night after night the thoughtful lady had stopped by to look in on him and to spoon him some hot broth. Old Hans had done the right thing, writing Anna Marie into his will the way he did. Such kindness should not go unrewarded.

Anna Marie could not have agreed more emphatically with such conversation. Although she may have been more interested in receiving the reward than in performing the kindness, she soon had a number of regulars she would look in on to administer her 'healing' broth.

Anna told her friends that she believed her mission in life was to make 'old folks from the Fatherland happy'. She felt that she wanted to do whatever she could to help ease their suffering. 'Think how terrible it must be to be all alone and sick in a strange land. I just want to help them to rest easy.'

And Anna Marie did just that. She helped one old gent after another to rest in peace – after seeing that she had been included in the old man's will, of course.

Ernest Kohler, who died in 1933, left Anna a fine office building. Advantageously for Anna's perverse purposes, a

Dr Arthur Vos had his medical office in the building. It was a simple matter for Anna Marie, in her role as landlord, to call upon the doctor and to steal several prescription blanks. These were necessary for the homework in which Anna was engaged. Her husband Philip complained about how she was certain to corrupt her mind spending her evenings reading books about crime, drugs, and poisons.

'First you complain when I go to the beer gardens at night,' Anna Marie answered with a scowl. 'Now you complain when I spend my evenings at home reading. So make up your mind!'

Philip was unaware that he served his spouse as a convenient guinea pig for her deadly concoctions.

'Take your medicine, *Liebchen*,' Anna Marie reminded him.

'More medicine!' Philip made a terrible face. 'Pardon my ingratitude, but why is it that I always feel worse after taking the medicine that you give me?'

'Don't be silly, you naughty boy,' Anna said as she laughed. 'Now take the medicine that Mama gives you.'

Twice Anna Marie had tried to insure Philip for $20,000. Each time the insurance company turned him down as a poor risk because of his ill health.

An insurance company's refusal to accept him quite probably saved his life. If Anna had been able to secure a sizeable policy on the long-suffering Philip, she would have quite likely decided to make him a victim rather than a guinea pig.

Anna Marie managed to obtain thirteen kinds of poisons and narcotics on the prescription blanks that she had pilfered from the office of Dr Vos. She sent her son to the pharmacy to purchase the poisons with the forged forms.

Greed proved to be the pretty poisoner's undoing. Not contented with the $45,000 that she had collected for 'making old folks comfortable' in an eight-year period, she began to move far too fast.

A sixty-eight-year-old gardener was dead the day after

POISONING

he was introduced to the curvy contralto folksinger. And within a few days, another of the elderly gentlemen Anna Marie 'looked in on' was found dead.

The Cincinnati police had long been puzzled by the rash of deaths of dysentery that had plagued elderly men in the German colony. Captain Patrick Haynes, chief of the Cincinnati police, ordered an autopsy of the two most recent deaths. He was hardly surprised to discover evidence of poison in their organs.

Anna Marie admitted that it was indeed a strange coincidence that so many of her charges had died of dysentery. But after all, she explained, so many elderly people had troubles with their bowels and intestines. Then, too, some older folks had never quite adjusted to life in America, especially the changes in foods, diet, and nutritional standards. Even the beer was different, you know.

Captain Haynes was one man who failed to succumb to Anna Marie Hahn's rationale. He ordered the other bodies of her 'patients' exhumed. Four different kinds of poisons were detected in the decomposed remains.

Anna Marie was also betrayed on the home front when the police confiscated Philip's newest bottle of 'medicine' and declared that it, too, revealed elements of poison when subjected to laboratory analyses.

The beautiful blonde angel of death exhibited little emotion in the courtroom. Even the most sympathetic reporter could hardly exercise enough literary license to term her attitude as a repentant one. But Anna Marie Hahn certainly made good copy, and she enjoyed reading every word the newspapers had to say about her.

Anna exerted the full power of her charm one last time when she prevailed upon the warden to allow her to throw a party in her death-row cell just two nights before her execution. The crime reporters were able to keep their promises to give her a good final writeup when she walked boldly to her death in the electric chair in May 1938.

CHAPTER FOURTEEN

RITUAL MURDERS

THE SECRET RELIGIOUS WAR OF A MURDEROUS MORMON SECT

A secret religious war is being conducted by a murderous Mormon sect which believes that killing a 'sinner' is the only way to deliver his soul to heaven. Gore-splattered followers of the creed of 'blood atonement' insist that they execute wayward members in God's name.

Some police officials believe that certain power-hungry religious leaders wish to take over other groups in order to gain their financial assets, their congregations, and their multiple wives. The more than twenty slayings inspired the violent and realistically bloody motion picture *Messenger of Death*, starring Charles Bronson.

Mormon historian Tom Green expressed his opinion that the killings have been partially motivated by religious beliefs and partially by the desire to get rid of the competition. 'But the twenty or so killings that have been noticed by the police and the public are only some of the deaths. A member of one splinter group told me that there have been at least a dozen other disappearances that have gone unreported since 1981.'

The web of murders centres on the now-deceased Ervil LeBaron, an excommunicated polygamist who declared himself to be God's prophet on Earth and assumed the title of 'The One Mighty and Strong'. In a book of 'New Covenants' that he hand-scrawled while he was in prison, LeBaron drew up a blueprint of death for 'traitors' – members of feuding sects in Utah, Arizona, Texas, California, and Mexico. LeBaron didn't undertake all the killings himself. He also had his fanatical followers, both men and women, to carry out the systematic assassinations.

Ervil was so ruthless that he had his pregnant daughter killed for disagreeing with him, and he ordered his brother Joel shot down to clear the path for his own bid to become God on Earth.

In October 1987, the man accused of Joel's execution, Daniel Ben Jordan, was himself gunned down. He had committed the fatal error of straying away from the protection of nine of his wives and twenty-one of his children while deer hunting.

Utah detective Lieutenant Paul Forbes revealed that Jordan's body was found in the southern part of the state. 'He had been shot in the head and chest with a 9mm handgun. We don't know who did it. Dan left camp and just didn't come back. Someone was waiting for him.'

The murder of Jordan, self-styled prophet-apostle of the Church of the Lamb of God, was another in a string of mysterious slayings that remain wrapped in a cloak of secrecy.

Lieutenant Forbes is said by many experts to be the United States's leading police authority on blood atonement groups. 'The Mormons practised polygamy until the late 1800s,' he explained, 'when Utah was trying to become a state. At this time, the Church opted to discontinue the practice of multiple wives. However, a number of groups broke off from the original Church and set up on their own. Each sect was led by an individual who claimed to have the "keys of authority" and a lot of the groups left Utah. They went to Mexico, Arizona, and California.'

One such group of fundamentalists who broke away from the Church of Jesus Christ of Latter Day Saints established themselves in Chihuahua, Mexico, and titled themselves 'Colonia Juarez'. Ervil LeBaron had been reared in this colony of polygamists, the son of a farmer who had been excommunicated from the mainstream faith in 1924 because of his bizarre beliefs and teachings. Ervil and his six brothers were, in turn, excommunicated in 1944.

Joel LeBaron, upon his father's death, announced that he possessed the Key of Power, and he founded the Church of the Firstborn of the Fullness of Time. Joel declared himself God's prophet, and demanded that all of his wishes be carried out and obeyed without question.

His brother Ervil wasn't so certain that Joel was correct, and since Ervil was in the enviable position of writing most of the sect's literature, he had the ability to set down the facts as he perceived them. He decided that Adam was God and that Joseph Smith, the founder of Mormonism, was the Holy Ghost. Ervil also declared that the doctrine of blood atonement demanded that all sinners be put to death. Furthermore, he envisioned that the One Mighty and Strong had supremacy over all Mormons.

Lieutenant Forbes said that Ervil sent out notes announcing that he was the final authority and that all group members must pay tithes to him. In 1970, Joel had had enough of such insubordination behind his back. He assessed Ervil as unstable and stripped him of his leadership in the sect. Undaunted, Ervil quickly founded the Church of the Lamb of God and announced that he was the genuine One Mighty and Strong. In short order he took thirteen wives and embarked on his crusade of blood.

Police authorities have established that from this point onward in the secret war, gory events occurred very rapidly.

August 1972: Joel LeBaron is murdered in Mexico by order of his brother.

December 1974: A squad of men and women on a commando-style raid firebomb the Mexican village of Los Molinos, a Mormon community. Two fundamentalists are killed; fifteen others are wounded. Ervil LeBaron is said to have led the attack.

RITUAL MURDERS

January 1975: Ervil decides that the wife of one of his followers, Naomi Zarate, is disobedient. Shortly thereafter, she disappears and is never seen again.

April 1975: Robert Simons of Grantsville, Utah, disputes Ervil's claim and declares himself the One Mighty and Strong. Simons vanishes and is presumed to have been executed.

June 1975: Dean Vest, one of Ervil's military chieftains, becomes sickened by the executions and murders and prepares to defect. He is murdered in his sleep.

March 1976: Ervil is arrested in Mexico for complicity in his brother Joel's death. His twelve-year sentence is abruptly reversed after eight months and he is released. While in prison, however, he converts new followers, including drug smuggler Leo Peter Evoniuk.

April 1977: Ervil announces to his followers that his daughter Rebecca has rebelled against him. He orders her strangled and buried in a hole in the mountains.

May 1977: Dr Rullon Allred, leader of the largest polygamist sect in Utah and Ervil's principal rival for the title of God's Prophet, is murdered in Murray, Utah. The assassins are identified as two young women followers of Ervil LeBaron.

LeBaron boldly dispatches a hit team to Allred's funeral, but the gunmen withdraw when they spot heavy police protection. They must flee to Texas to escape Ervil's wrath for their failed mission.

May 1979: Ervil is arrested by Mexican police, extradited to Utah, tried and convicted for the murder of Allred and for a machine-gun attack on his brother Verlan LeBaron.

August 1981: Ervil LeBaron is found dead in his cell at Utah state prison. The official report lists the cause of his death as a heart attack.

August 1981: Verlan LeBaron is killed in a mysterious car crash in Mexico.

July 1984: Brenda Lafferty and her baby daughter Erica, fifteen months, are found dead, victims of a ritual killing at their home in American Fork, Utah. Their throats are found to be so deeply slashed that their heads were almost severed.

May 1987: Leo Peter Evoniuk, fifty-two, presiding patriarch of the Millennial Church of Jesus Christ, vanishes while making a business call near Watsonville, California. He leaves behind only some blood, his dentures, and several 9mm shell casings.

October 1987: Daniel Ben Jordan, fifty-three, prophet apostle of the Church of the Lamb of God, is ambushed while deer hunting in southern Utah.

Lieutenant Forbes hastened to clarify that the people conducting the bloody secret war 'are like clan chieftains, not like the rest of the Mormons'. Most of the polygamous Mormons, the police authority emphasized, are law-abiding and low-key people who do not wish to make waves of any kind.

'Groups like Ervil LeBaron's and the ones it spawned are different. There are about ten of them in the south-western states and Mexico. Some are quite wealthy. Some, like the remains of Ervil's, are destitute. They are very secretive, very close.

'We estimate that there are thirty thousand people involved in these groups,' Lieutenant Forbes concluded, 'and the power struggles between them are held to see who can take over the other's financial base.'

Historian Tom Green adds: 'These are struggles to get rid of the opposition. They know if they kill all the rival prophets that a lot of the undecided followers will come to them – because they're the only ones left.'

A WEIRD UNSOLVED MURDER CASE – THE BLOODY BLACK MAGIC DEATHS OF THE HEALER AND HIS FAMILY

There is a shadow of the Dark Ages upon this crime, which has eluded solution by the most competent of investigators. Yet the events in this account did not occur in a lonely cabin on a barren island, but in the heart of one of the most industrial and sophisticated of American cities.

It was a little before midnight on 2 July 1929 and in the centre of Detroit, Michigan, lights still blazed. But in that part of the city known as Little Italy, most sources of illumination had been extinguished, for the inhabitants were hardworking folk who retired early.

The day had been a hot one, but seemingly on the very stroke of midnight, a welcome breeze stirred the trees on St Aubin Avenue. A patrolman passed down the sidewalk and turned into the police station on the corner to make his report that all was well.

Dominic Diapolo, who kept the delicatessen on the avenue, was always the last tradesman to close his shop: at about 11:30 p.m., he came out of the premises and glanced up and down the street to assure himself that no more customers were approaching.

Diapolo rather idly observed that lights were still burning at 3587 next door, but that was nothing unusual, for his neighbour, Benjamino Evangelista, always kept late hours.

Evangelista was an enigma not only to Diapolo but to many of the other local residents who had known him in Italy before they emigrated to the States. Evangelista had been born in Cassino, which stands in a district of rugged mountains, where the rural folk still lived in thought and in habit several generations behind the city dwellers.

In 1914, when he was twenty-nine, Evangelista left this primitive district for America. He rapidly acquired fluency in the language and soon found work as a carpenter. He blended into his new environment very well, and nobody noticed anything unusual for many months – until he suddenly revealed himself as a prophet and a healer.

Often Evangelista would pray fervently in the middle of his work, and one day when one of his workmates cut himself badly, Evangelista promptly stopped the flow of blood from an artery by saying a few words over the wound in a language unknown to his companions. It now became clear to his co-workers that Evangelista had occult powers.

Diapolo of the delicatessen didn't believe that his neighbour was so divinely gifted. But when Mrs Vaniel Vetrando, who lived near by, told him that Evangelista had cured her ailing infant by making strange signs in the air over the child and reading in a peculiar language from a book, Diapolo began to have second thoughts.

Later, when a woman named Santina, who was dying of consumption, was carried on a stretcher to Evangelista's house, the carpenter agreed to heal her, but only if she would marry him. Although she was too weak to rise from the bed in which she had been placed, the desperate woman agreed to the conditions.

As soon as Santina had become Mrs Evangelista, she staged a rapid recovery. As the years passed, she bore him four children. There were three girls – Angeline, Matilda, and Jenny – and a boy – Morrio.

Evangelista flourished and became a master carpenter and plumber. And after long hours of hard work, he would attend his patients, for not only members of the local Italian community came to be healed, but many others sought him out when their conventional doctors failed them. Evangelista never turned anyone away. He burned midnight oil calculating horoscopes, studying occultism, or brewing potions from the herbs that he grew in his garden.

Father Francis Beccherini, a local Roman Catholic priest, tried to persuade Evangelista to abandon occultism, but he refused. The priest alleged that it was sad that one blessed with the gift of healing and with such fine children should be so cursed by a need to study the occult.

So stood the story until that terrible night of 2 July 1929, when it seemed as if a black cloud of evil descended upon Detroit and lingered over St Aubin Avenue.

That night, as best the events can be reconstructed, Evangelista saw his wife and children to bed, then returned to his study on the ground floor to check the proofs of a bizarre book that he had authored. Friends had heard him say it would be his Bible, and he had entitled it *The Oldest History of the World Revealed by Occult Sciences*. Behind him, as he sat at his desk, was an altar, and to the left and right were stacks of books, astrological charts, and chemical apparatus. He had not locked the front door, but his study door was closed. Evangelista worked on as night enveloped the city, and Little Italy slept unconscious of the evil that was about to visit St Aubin Avenue.

It was not until abut 11:00 a.m. on 3 July that Vincent Elias called at Evangelista's home and raised the curtain on a crime that stunned and nauseated the entire city. Getting no reply as he knocked at the front door, Elias entered the silent house and called a cheery greeting at the door to Evangelista's study.

Elias's next words froze on his lips, for the study resembled a slaughterhouse. Evangelista's decapitated body was slumped on his scattered proof sheets. His head lay on the floor.

Babbling incoherently, Elias sought Diapolo, who phoned the police. Patrolmen Costage and Lawrence from Hunt Street station arrived and immediately saw what Elias in his horror had missed – a trail of small bloody footprints leading upstairs.

Here, the police officers discovered, the horror continued. Mrs Evangelista and her four children had been butchered, decapitated and disembowelled.

Later, when additional officers arrived at the scene, a search of the house revealed nearly a dozen macabre life-sized waxen figures dangling from the ceiling of a curtained-off room in the basement. Each figure bore the grotesque face of a devil.

Doctors called to the scene of the hideous slaughter theorized that the murderer must have had considerable strength for his size, for bloody footprints revealed that the killer wore only size five shoes. The mortal wounds had been caused by either a scimitar, a sabre, a machete, or some similar weapon.

Because none of the nearby neighbours had heard the Evangelistas' dogs barking during the night, it was suggested that the murderer must have been known to the family and to their canine guardians. Continuing further along such lines, it was theorized that perhaps a disgruntled patient of Evangelista's healing skills had committed the grisly deed. Investigation proved such a theory without foundation, for the healer and his family appeared to have been very well liked by all those whom he had treated with his unconventional medicine.

When women's lingerie was found in a cellar room, police authorities thought that the slain occultist may have engaged in some sort of devil worship that debauched females. This hypothesis was rapidly exploded when former patients explained that Evangelista required a garment that had been worn next to the skin when he performed the healing rites that in almost all cases restored them to health.

After every possible trail the police followed ended up in a dead end, Inspector Fred Frahm began to get interested in Evangelista's manuscript for his *Oldest History of the World*. Once he had read a few passages from the strange work, the detective expressed his belief that the book might prove more revelatory and productive than following up leads about neighbourhood vendettas and the like.

There was a macabre, exalted madness about the script, and the mystery deepened when Frahm remembered that one of the little daughters had had one of her arms cut off at the shoulder, for he read in Evangelista's 'Bible' the following words:

> If any Caion men would acquaint themselves with Caion or Aliel women, they would be cut to pieces and fed to the slaves ... Berland began to run away from him, but blood came out of her shoulder and she couldn't magnetize the people any longer.

Had not the entire Evangelista family been cut to pieces? Had not little Angeline's arm been severed at the shoulder?

The printer of the weird 'history', Francis Slunder, of 3652 Meldrum Avenue, Detroit, was traced. But he could throw no light on the meaning of the book.

Fortuna J. Martin, the manufacturer of the eerie devil figures, was located at the Johnson Flag and Decorating Company of 3529 Gratiot Avenue, Detroit. Martin told police that Evangelista had instructed him to make the devil figures as grotesque as possible. It was Martin's understanding that Evangelista wanted the wax demons for a motion picture that he intended to film. Martin added that his customer seemed sane enough – until religion was mentioned.

All the known occultists of Detroit were arrested on suspicion. Psychic readers and Spiritualist mediums were brought in for hours of unproductive questioning.

Museums and arms collectors were visited, but the murder weapon was never discovered or even identified.

Utterly baffled, the detectives then decided to consult the various mediums and occultists for psychic guidance on the mystery, but they learned nothing that they didn't already know.

James E. Chenot, prosecuting attorney, launched a campaign to drive all mediums, psychic sensitives, and occultists from Detroit, but when it was revealed that the police themselves were consulting the seers, the drive collapsed.

Months later, a desperate theorist suggested that Evangelista himself might have murdered his family, so the authorities had his body exhumed and his fingerprints taken. This theory, of course, did not explain who, then, would have slain and decapitated Evangelista after he butchered his family. The police were, by that time, so obsessed with the hunt for the murderer that they had almost reached the stage where they might even have theorized that Evangelista had not only murdered his family, but he cut off his own head afterwards and disposed of the weapon by means of black magic.

'The Evangelista murders,' said one of the chief detectives, 'constitute one of the most unique cases police were ever called on to handle anywhere. Not only were the murders singularly frightful, but there was an element about them that removed them from the modern world. This is a case in which a murderer from the Dark Ages has baffled a thoroughly modernized police force, though every means known to criminal science was employed to detect him.'

Were Benjamino Evangelista and his family the victims of a very bloody vendetta set in motion by person or persons unknown? Or had Evangelista somehow managed to conjure up a demonic denizen from some nether region? Who can say?

CHAPTER FIFTEEN

ROBBERY

BANDIT IS TOLD HE CANNOT COMPLETE HOLDUP UNLESS HE HAS AN ACCOUNT AT THE BANK

We've all heard those cold words at one time or another: 'I'm sorry, I cannot cash your cheque unless you have an account with our bank.'

Al Camili, a would-be bank robber, heard the icy, professionally uttered brush-off under the most stressful of circumstances – while he was trying to rob the bank!

In October of 1990, Camili handed a stickup note to a teller at a downtown Albany, New York, bank. The teller carefully read his demand for cash, then replied that she could not hand over any money to him unless he had an account with the bank.

Totally nonplussed, Camili left the teller's window and ran from the bank empty-handed.

Pressured to robbery by an unrelenting cocaine habit, Camili felt he had no choice other than to try it again ten days later.

He no doubt felt a sinking feeling in his stomach, a presentiment of defeat, when he found himself approaching the same teller who had previously rejected his demand for money.

In this instance when he presented her with the stickup note, she simply turned and walked away from him.

Stung by the ultimate in silent rejections, Camili once again fled the bank without the loot. He realized that there was no course of action open to him other than to do what he had done before: rob the bank located across the street. The tellers there were much more compliant and co-operative.

Al Camili was arrested for robbery a few days later, and a police spokesperson stated that the hapless thief had confessed to three completed bank robberies – and two *attempted* bank thefts.

A SORDID SECRET LIFE – MINISTER STEALS FIFTY THOUSAND DOLLARS TO PAY FOR HIS LUST FOR HOOKERS

When the pastor of a Detroit area church was arrested in January of 1991, police officials revealed that he was accused of robbing fourteen banks of $50,000 and spending all the money on wild sexual encounters with hookers.

After the police had nailed him for robbing two banks on 9 January, a law-enforcement spokesperson said that the errant man of the cloth had at first been suspected of having spent some of the money on his church. But sadly, according to the FBI, the minister had confessed to having robbed twelve other banks in the Detroit area and of having blown all $50,000 on cheap street prostitutes and high-priced call girls. The pastor admitted to an insatiable appetite for sex.

The minister, who is married and has a small daughter, was identified as the infamous 'bearded bank bandit', whose picture had been taken by bank video cameras in many of the robberies. The pastor began his crime spree in September of 1989. He never used a weapon, but simply handed tellers a note and kept one hand menacingly in a coat pocket.

The cleric, who had served for eight years as pastor of a church in a suburb of Detroit, resigned his post in mid-

January. After the emotional farewell service, the pastor and his wife received hugs of comfort from compassionate church members, and he asked for their prayers in the days ahead.

Church officials affirmed that the pastor had been extremely well respected as a minister. He had lived with his family in a modest bungalow, and both he and his wife drove older model cars. Neither of them appeared interested in anything other than a quiet and unobtrusive life style.

Stunned by his colleague's secret dark side, a fellow clergyman told the media that the prodigal pastor was an impeccable citizen, a good minister, and a very good father. All those who knew the man were stunned.

The pastor was released on bail, but he can face up to twenty years in prison and a $250,000 fine on each charge.

AT BIT OF HEAVEN YOGURT SHOP – THIEF GETS RELIGION INSTEAD OF LOOT

In October of 1990, ex-con Matt Davis walked into the Bit of Heaven Yogurt Shop in La Jolla, California, intent on robbery – but he found Christ instead of cash.

Pretty Bible student Amy Kerns was minding the store when Davis ordered a yogurt and gave her a five-dollar bill attached to a note that informed her that he was robbing the shop and that she must hand over every cent in the cash register.

Amy didn't see a knife or a gun on Davis, but she did see the desperation in his eyes.

She opened the cash register so that he would know that she was complying with his demands, and she gave him the one hundred dollars in the drawer.

In a soft and gentle voice, Amy, a student at a local Bible

college, asked Davis why he was so troubled, so desperate that he would steal.

Davis began to open to the attractive yogurt dispenser, who had now opened her Bible and was beginning to dispense scriptural passages of comfort. He told her that he had just been released from jail to face a huge stack of debts. He had been searching for work all week, but he was unable to find a job. His wife and two kids had left him and he missed them so much that he thought he would go crazy.

Amy and the holdup man sat talking for over an hour. When customers came into the shop, he allowed her to wait on them, but she had no change. Davis returned all but ten dollars to the cash drawer. 'I've got to keep a few bucks,' he pleaded.

When customers would leave the shop, Amy would return to Davis to provide him with more heavenly advice. Over and over she reminded him that God would change his life if only he would permit Him to enter his heart.

Finally Matt Davis left the yogurt shop with a promise that he would return later.

The ex-convict's tale of woes had touched her heart, but Amy called the police on the strong recommendation of a friend, who convinced her that she did not really know the deeds of which Davis might be capable. His next victim might not be so fortunate as to have a Bible close at hand.

Although Amy Kerns suffered from feelings of betrayal, Davis, upon his arrest, stated that he held no bitterness towards her. He informed his attorney that he was glad that Amy had helped him to find God and to discover that there were people like Amy in the world who would help him change his life.

GUNMEN PLACE BABY IN MICROWAVE OVEN TO FORCE GRANDFATHER TO OPEN HIS SAFE

It is always a sad and tragic affair when the objects of technology that have been designed and manufactured to serve humankind can be perverted into terrible tools of torture, torment and death.

Most of us have heard the sick joke about the children who placed the pet cat into the microwave oven to dry it off so their mother would not punish them for getting the pussycat wet. Such a childish application of microwave technology would, of course, cause the animal to explode, literally cooked from the inside out.

The very thought of placing a child inside a microwave oven stretches beyond the furthest perimeters of bad taste into a taboo area that even the sickest of sick jokes would not violate. Yet on 26 September 1990, three gunmen performed such an unspeakable deed when they put the granddaughter of Sergio Gonzalez in a microwave oven to force him to open his safe.

Shortly after midnight, three ski-masked thugs jumped Gonzalez, forty-nine, in the Soundview section of the Bronx. Gonzalez who describes himself as a 'policy operator', was returning home with his wife, Beatrice; his daughter-in-law, Hope; and his nine-year-old daughter, Monica, when three men with Uzi sub-machine-guns ran at them.

When Gonzalez began struggling with one of the hoodlums, another thug fired a blast from the Uzi that tore through his wife's jacket and shirt and missed the side of her chest by an eighth of an inch.

Later, Sergio Gonzalez would declare his wife's narrow escape from a fatal bullet wound to be a miracle, but he was unaware that a second miracle was also occurring at that very moment: a neighbour had heard the sounds of scuffling and gunfire and had dialled the 911 emergency number.

Sergio surrendered the $4,000 that he had on him, but the hoodlums were convinced that he had more cash hidden away in a safe inside his house.

Forcing entry, the gunmen rounded up Gonzalez's sons, Sergio, Jr., thirteen, and Stephen, twelve, tied up all six members of the family; and, in Sergio's words, 'got mean'. When he refused to go upstairs to open the safe, they hit and kicked various members of his family and shoved the tip of the barrel of an Uzi in his eye.

When none of the rough stuff prompted the desired results of coercing the head of the household into surrendering the contents of his safe, one of the men picked up Monique, the baby granddaughter who had been crying out in fear, and placed her in a microwave oven.

Gonzalez stared in disbelief. No one could be so cruel, so desperate, so inhuman.

Then the hoodlum closed the door on little Monique.

Sergio knew that it would not take long for the baby to suffocate in the oven and to die – even without the power turned on. He quickly agreed to yield the money in the upstairs safe, and the gunmen ran up the stairs after him.

It was while the three thugs in the ski masks were happily scooping up more bills from the safe – $3,000 worth – that Sergio Gonzalez managed to turn the tables on his attackers. Their attention diverted by their greed, he slipped out of the room and barricaded himself in an upstairs bedroom.

Meanwhile, on the lower floor, Beatrice had managed to lock a door that would trap the three gunmen upstairs.

And it was at that most propitious moment that the police arrived in answer to the 911 call. Officer Patrick Moore and his partner, Gabriel Osorio, entered the Gonzalez dwelling with their weapons drawn and discovered the family members tied up and lying on the living-room floor.

Hearing noises coming from upstairs, the investigating

officers could hear the three gunmen trying desperately to pry off the iron bars on the windows so that they might make their escape.

Realizing police officers were downstairs, the hoodlums tried one last scam: they discarded the loot, their guns, their ski masks, and their bulletproof vests and came downstairs pretending to be robbery victims who had been ensnared by the Gonzalez family.

Officers Moore and Osorio did not buy the routine.

The three men were arrested on weapons, assault, and robbery charges, as well as two attempted murder charges.

MEDICAL SCHOOL DROPOUT HEEDS MURDEROUS VOICES, ROBS BANKS TO FINANCE ASSASSINATIONS OF REAGAN AND BUSH

John S. Daughetee, thirty-five, began hearing the evil voices during his second year at the University of Utah Medical School. He dropped out of school in 1986 after he attempted suicide and was diagnosed as a paranoid schizophrenic.

In November 1986, while he was living in a Sacramento hotel, the voices from unseen entities spoke to him again and ordered him to kill President Reagan. The invisible murderous mentors instructed him to take a bus to Los Angeles, purchase a rifle, and make his way to the Reagans' ranch near Santa Barbara.

Fortunately, Daughetee had confided in some of his relatives and had informed them of the mission on which his voices had sent him. Members of Daughetee's family managed to talk him out of the plot, and they convinced him to enter a Veterans' Administration hospital.

The voices refused to yield to psychiatric therapy, and

two years later, Daughetee was sent on another assignment to assassinate President Ronald Reagan.

In September of 1988, he acquired a small apartment in Flint, Michigan, because he was aware that presidential candidates George Bush and Michael Dukakis would be campaigning a great deal in Detroit, and he knew that such steady political activity would eventually bring President Reagan to the area.

In December, he bought a .22-calibre handgun and began to rob banks. He had to earn a living, after all. He could not live in his apartment for free, and he did have to eat. In addition, he had to travel a great deal to maintain a steady surveillance on Reagan. Robbing banks seemed the most practical method of financing the ambitious mission that the voices had assigned to him.

As Daughetee criss-crossed the nation stalking Reagan and his successor, George Bush, he held up banks in San Francisco, Portland, Baltimore, Sacramento, Miami, and Charlotte, North Carolina.

When Bush moved into the Oval Office, the voices presented Daughetee with a new priority, and he did his utmost to get within pistol range of the new President of the United States. He followed Bush's itinerary of scheduled appearances in the nation's capital, and he even staked out what he believed to be the President's favourite restaurants. FBI agents later determined that Daughetee had followed Bush through eight states.

On 17 April 1989 Daughetee began to stake out the Detroit-area town of Hamtramck. Ten days before a rally there for Bush, the voices instructed him to purchase a more powerful handgun. He went to Guns Galore in Flint and bought a .380-calibre pistol.

Three days before the Hamtramck rally, Daughetee moved his base of operations into the nearby Presidential Inn and carefully surveyed the area where President George Bush would deliver a speech to a crowd of about four thousand people. The voices told him to buy a new suit and a trench coat so he would look like a Secret Service agent and blend in with the crowd.

During his careful surveillance of the area, Daughetee had spotted a burned-out house that would position him within two hundred yards of Bush. He stood there during the President's speech, levelling his .380-calibre pistol again and again at the figure on the dais. He assessed the situation as presenting him with a 'rough shot', but he was convinced that he 'could have got him'.

Thankfully, the voices did not pronounce the final order to kill on that April day in 1989, and Daughetee did not pull the trigger.

On 4 August 1989 he was arrested within moments after having robbed Gateway Savings in Oakland, California, with a pellet gun. He was indicted for the Oakland robbery, and he admitted to having held up eight banks in order to finance his cross-country assassination plots against Presidents Reagan and Bush. Under a plea-bargaining agreement, Daughetee pleaded guilty to five of the eight robberies, and the charges of the other holdups were dismissed.

It is most fortunate that Daughetee was apprehended at last, for he informed police investigators that the voices had recently instructed him to begin to kill schoolchildren to compensate for his failed efforts to assassinate a president.

In January 1990, Assistant US Attorney Mark Zanides issued a press statement indicating that Daughetee's revelations to police authorities painted 'a chilling portrait of a seriously disturbed and violent man'.

Richard McDrew, chief of the Secret Service in San Francisco, said, 'We consider him someone to be concerned about if he got out – not a John Hinckley [the would-be assassin of Ronald Reagan], but in that class. We consider it very serious.'

In his motion requesting psychiatric tests for the prisoner, Zanides said that the police had achieved the goal of protecting the President 'or anyone else' from the power of the murderous voices that had for so long controlled the tragic life of John S. Daughetee.

GROCERY CLERK FOILS ARMED ROBBERY BY BUYING BANDIT'S HOLDUP GUNS

On a chilly night in January 1990, grocery clerk Frank Alvarez was in the process of closing the Super Food Market in Abilene, Texas, when the sole remaining customer in the store ran to the counter, pulled out two revolvers, and yelled at Alvarez and the other clerk to hand over all the money in the cash register.

Alvarez remembered that his mind reeled with the tension of the situation. As he looked into the barrels of two revolvers, he tried to consider the odds as calmly as possible. If he resisted, the hoodlum could shoot both of them and take the money. If he complied, the bandit could blast both of them into oblivion after he had the cash.

Perhaps Alvarez will never know where he received the inspiration for what he did next, but it certainly ranks as one of the most daring gambles taken while staring in the eyes of death ever recorded in the annals of weird crime.

'Sir,' Alvarez asked the robber, 'why don't you sell me one of your guns if you need money so badly?'

Such a seemingly wiseacre question from the victim of a holdup could have brought about a pistol-whipping at best, instant death at worst. Incredibly, though, Alvarez had gained the thief's attention.

'Why do you need two guns to hold up a store?' the grocery clerk wanted to know. 'One should be enough. Why not sell one of the guns to me? It is clear to see that I need protection.'

Fantastic as it may seem, the two-gunned robber began to think over the proposition. 'How much would you give me?' he scowled at Alvarez.

The clerk placed one hundred dollars on the counter. The bandit kept his other gun trained on the two employees, but he took the cash and placed a revolver on the counter.

His heart thudding in his chest, Alvarez decided to press his luck. Once again he argued that if the man was so desperate for cash, he would also buy the other pistol from him for the same amount of money.

For one terrible moment it appeared that Frank Alvarez had indeed gone too far.

'I think you are trying to pull something on me!' the bandit roared suspiciously.

Fighting to retain his calm, Alvarez insisted that such was not the case. 'No, I am not trying to "pull something" on you. I need two guns. One for me, and one for my helper in the store. We both need a gun.'

As Alvarez placed another hundred dollars on the counter, he also used the motion to cover his pushing of a button that locked the front doors to the Super Food Market.

Either the bandit was basically an honest person who really did not wish to enter a life of crime or he was the most inept holdup man in the history of criminal encounters, for he tossed his second revolver on the counter, snatched the money, and ran for the front doors.

Alvarez remembered that the thief slammed into the locked doors with a 'tremendous noise'. Dazed, it took him a few moments before he realized that escape into the Abilene streets was not going to be that easy.

'Let me outa here!' he demanded. 'Open the doors!'

The revolvers were now in Alvarez's hands. 'Throw down the money,' the grocery clerk told the bamboozled bandit, 'and I'll let you go.'

Desperately, the thug threw the money on the floor, and Alvarez pushed the button that opened the locked doors. The would-be robber then made his escape into the night – minus his two revolvers *and* the money that he had earned by selling them to Frank Alvarez.

A spokesperson from the Abilene Police commented that the bizarre scenario that had occurred at the Super Food

Market was the most unusual robbery incident in his experience or in his memory.

Apparently agreeing with Alvarez's assessment that the hoodlum had been 'stupid, naïve, or stoned – or all three,' the police spokesperson added that 'you couldn't consider him a brain surgeon'.

'GERALDO MADE ME DO IT!' COUPLE ROB BANK AFTER LEARNING HOW FROM TALK SHOW

Elizabeth Lange and her boyfriend David Marx were watching the 12 December 1990 segment of the *Geraldo Rivera* show about thieves and bank robbers when Dave commented how easy it seemed to be to pull off a heist.

To hear the panel of expert criminals talk about it on television, robbing a bank seemed so simple that the young couple decided to do it.

On Friday 15 December, Elizabeth and Dave walked into a bank in Miami, Florida, and handed a teller a note demanding money. And then, just as easy as the panel of thieves had described the procedure on Rivera's television programme, they walked out with $2,125.

Elizabeth Lange surrendered to the police on Saturday 16 December, but 'Dave', her sweetheart and accomplice, remained at large.

The nineteen-year-old first-timer could face twenty years in prison for bank robbery. Florida legal observers wisecracked that her attorney will probably initiate the 'Geraldo' defence.

THE HOODLUM WHO INVENTED THE 'MICKEY FINN' KNOCKOUT DROPS

He was a cheap, two-bit hoodlum who made his living rolling drunks, but he managed to get his moniker in the dictionary as the name synonymous with a drink that has been drugged – a 'Mickey' or a 'Mickey Finn'.

Michael Finn really hit upon a gold mine. The stocky little bartender first bought his 'speciality' from a renegade voodoo doctor named Hall, who worked the joints on Chicago's rough Whiskey Row in the 1890s. The man had called it 'chloral hydrate', but it was soon to gain the name of its most notorious user – Mickey Finn.

After a customer had been drugged, Mickey would complain loudly to the other patrons in the Lone Star Saloon about those guys 'who couldn't hold their liquor'. Then he would don his derby hat and drag the victim off into the back room to 'sober up'. To the regular employees of the establishment, the back room was called the 'operating room', for it was here that Finn and his busty wife, Kate Rose, would strip an unconscious man of anything valuable before dumping him in the alley.

Mickey Finn had come up on the hard side of life. Even before he hit Chicago in 1890, he had a reputation for being one of the roughest little men in the Midwest. He had a job working for a saloon owner called Toronto Jim, and though Finn had originally been slated to tend bar, his quarrelsome nature and his quick fists soon earned him the position of bouncer.

Finn liked his work too well for Toronto Jim. The bar owner let the feisty Irishman go after a fight in which Mickey gouged out a customer's eye with a corkscrew over a sixty-cent tab.

Back on the street, Mickey built up a stake rolling drunks and picking pockets until he had enough saved to buy the Lone Star Saloon outright. With both legal and illegal businesses booming, he later invested in the Palm Gardens. Mickey's drug concoction had become famous in the underworld, but Finn himself had established a reputation for being the best fence in Chicago, and the finest stolen goods always passed through his hands.

Finn seemed impregnable. The Southside police were liberally supplied with good cigars, and they could always count on a little extra cash if they needed it. City politicians, such as Hinky Dink Michael Kenna and Bathhouse John Coughlin, counted on his connections to make certain that the ballot boxes were liberally spiked with enough votes to bring them back to their chairs at the city council table.

A woman proved to be Mickey Finn's undoing. In 1903, a barfly named Gold-Tooth Mary offered to buy the Lone Star from him. Finn looked at the woman as if she were crazy, then flatly refused her offer.

Gold-Tooth Mary had her heart set on owning that saloon. She flew into a rage, pulled a hat pin from her purse, and jabbed it through the little bartender's hand before she stormed out the door.

Later the woman testified before a city commission that was investigating crime in Chicago, and none of Finn's friends could help him when his liquor licence was revoked by the mayor. The doors of Finn's two thriving establishments were closed permanently in the winter of 1903.

Mickey Finn spent the remainder of his life peddling the drug that had earned his name. The last time that he came before the public eye was in 1918, when Chicago police caught him selling booze without a licence and running a disorderly house.

From that date onward, the man himself faded into obscurity, but his name, Mickey Finn, has remained as his legacy to the American vocabulary.

WRINKLED, WEATHERED 'RAMBO' STORMS LONDON BANK

It might have seemed like a good idea at the time – on that summer's day in 1992 – but the weathered and wrinkled 'Rambo' who approached the teller's window at a London bank began to sense that he must appear much more like a Hallowe'en trickster than a threatening robber.

'Gimme all your cash, Miss, and give me no trouble,' he snarled in his most menacing manner, hitching up his trousers in one of Jimmy Cagney's tough-guy mannerisms.

The pert young teller smiled at the elderly gentleman before her. He had to be pushing ninety if he had lived a day – and he definitely had to be joking with her. 'I beg pardon, sir,' she said, stifling a giggle. 'Do you have an account with our branch?'

'I told you to give me all your cash and no trouble,' he repeated, trying for a deeper-voiced snarl. 'Be quick about it, hear?'

The teller sniffed haughtily at the customer's tone of voice, then narrowed her eyes to study him more closely. He wore an army-surplus camouflage shirt with matching trousers. A thick belt appeared to hold a large knife and two hand grenades. He probably borrowed some toy weapons from his grandkids, she theorized. Must be some kinky World War II look the old folks were into.

When he pulled out the pistol, however, her eyes widened with genuine concern and no small degree of fear.

'Gimme the cash before I use this!' He spat out the words with great authority – but he could feel himself becoming short of breath.

By now one of the other tellers had noticed the elderly gentleman waving the pistol and had pressed the alarm button.

Flustered, the robber placed the pistol back in its holster.

His breath was coming in short, rapid, rasping gasps. There seemed no course open but to make a break for the door.

He might have made it, but a touch of gout in his right foot slowed him down; and by the time he reached the door, it seemed as though a veritable battalion of police officers was waiting for him.

It was at that point that witnesses in the bank saw the wrinkled Rambo drop to his knees and cry out in a voice that had by now been reduced to a croak: 'Don't hurt me! It's my heart... my heart! I've got a bum ticker. A bad heart problem. Three days ago I was on oxygen.'

Police investigation revealed that the would-be Rambo bank robber was a seventy-four-year-old love-sick senior citizen who had outfitted himself with a pistol, two hand grenades, and a knife and set out to rob a bank in order to acquire funds to pay for his girlfriend's hip replacement surgery.

Amazingly, in this case, justice truly was blind – and kind. When the London judge heard the would-be bank robber's side of the story, he gave him a suspended sentence.

CHAPTER SIXTEEN

SADISM

THE BLOODY BITE OF REAL-LIFE VAMPIRES

On Monday 15 January 1991, the day following the premiere of the new *Dark Shadows* television series featuring actor Ben Cross as vampire Barnabas Collins, a bearded man grabbed a forty-two-year-old woman in a library parking lot in Missoula, Montana, cut her neck, then kissed the open wound.

A Missoula police detective explained that the man had demanded money. The woman had complied and given him two dollars.

'Then he pulled her hair back, cut her with some kind of sharp object, kissed the wound, said, "Thank you," and fled on foot.'

The detective stated that the grisly vampire bandit was the object of an intense manhunt in Montana.

In February of 1991, a lesbian lover of a vampire was found guilty of murder in an Australian court trial. After deliberating for forty-eight hours, the jury convicted Annette Hall of murdering Charles Reilly in a coastal suburb and sentenced her to life in prison.

By her own testimony, Ms Hall stated that she had stalked and killed Reilly so her vampire lover, Susi Hampton, could drink his blood. She described in detail how her lesbian girlfriend went into a 'feeding frenzy' after Reilly had been stabbed over a dozen times.

Ms Hampton, a self-confessed vampire who lived on human blood, had previously pleaded guilty and had been sentenced to life in prison.

For Anne Rice, author of such novels as *Interview with the Vampire*, the vampire is a 'romantic, enthralling' figure. She perceives the vampire's image to be that of a 'person who never dies... takes a blood sacrifice in order to live, and exerts a charm over people; [the vampire is] a handsome, alluring, seductive person who captivates us, then drains the life out of us so that he or she can live. We long to be one of them and the idea of being sacrificed to them becomes rather romantic.'

Ms Rice is certainly not alone in her appraisal of the effect of the vampire of fiction to be a largely romantic one. The sexual metaphors to be found in the cinematic and literary portrayals of the vampire's seductive bite are many, and Anne Rice has touched a responsive, atavistic chord in her many enthusiastic readers.

While the sexual symbolism may be sensually appealing when we observe a sophisticated Count Dracula or a cultured and stylish Barnabas Collins emerge from the shadows and bite their beautiful victims' bare throats, the bloody accounts of real-life vampires reveal that they seldom operate with such dignity and poetry.

A classic example is that of Italy's Vincent Verzini, whose vampiric crimes were committed during the years between 1867 and 1871. The sexual nature of the twenty-two-year-old Verzini's acts is unmistakable. He achieved orgasm, it is reported, by grasping his female victim by the throat, first choking her, and then tearing her flesh with his teeth. He then proceeded to suck the blood through the wound.

One day pretty Maria Previtali, a nineteen-year-old cousin of Verzini, went out into the fields to work. Suddenly she became aware of footsteps other than her own. Frightened, she looked over her shoulder. Vincent was following.

Maria's footsteps picked up speed as she fought back waves of fear and panic. She thought of fourteen-year-old Johanna Motta, who had been viciously murdered the preceding December as she travelled on foot to a nearby village.

She remembered how she had lain awake that night, too frightened to sleep, and listened to Papa as he told her mother of the incident. '*Si*, Mama,' he had said, his voice filled with emotion, 'her throat was black and blue, and her mouth was full of dirt. All of her clothes were ripped off and her thighs were bloody with teeth marks. Her belly was cut wide open, and her insides were pulled out. And the parts that make her a woman had been torn right off!'

With such a memory to goad her, Maria shuddered and began to run. She recalled Mrs Frigeni, who had gone out to work in the fields one morning, and by nightfall, had still not returned. When her husband had gone out to look for her, he found her naked and mutilated body. She had been strangled with a leather thong and flesh had been torn from her abdomen.

Maria was almost breathless now. She could run no more. Her footsteps faltered, and two powerful hands grabbed her.

She felt herself thrown to the ground. Fingers like bands of steel closed around her throat. She could not even scream. It was a miracle that saved her.

She started to faint, and the hasty vampire relaxed his grip. Drawing in her breath, the courageous girl brought up her knee and kicked her insane cousin in the stomach.

As he staggered backward, Maria sprang to her feet, rubbing her burning throat. 'Vincent,' she gasped, 'are you crazy? Are you trying to kill me?'

Maria's blow had temporarily drained the vampire of his blood lust. He muttered obscenities, then walked off across the field.

Maria ran home, told her horrified mother of the attack, and was taken at once to the village prefect. Verzini was immediately arrested, and after being questioned at length, made a full and detailed confession. He was tried, convicted, and sentenced to life imprisonment.

Although Verzini's examiners found 'no evidence of psychosis', there can be little doubt that his vampirism was the expression of deep derangement and sexual perversion. That such was the case is shown lucidly in Verzini's own words:

'I had an unspeakable delight in strangling women, experiencing during the act erections and real sexual pleasure. The feeling of pleasure while strangling them was much greater than that which I experienced while masturbating.

'I took great delight in drinking Motta's blood. It also gave me great pleasure to pull the hairpins out of the hair of my victims.

'It never occurred to me to touch or to look at the genitals . . . It satisfied me to seize the women by the neck and suck their blood.'

Not manifestly sexual were the vampirish acts of John Haigh, British killer of nine. Haigh's thirst for human blood is believed by some authorities to have been somehow linked to his religious fanaticism.

Haigh was obsessed with the Old Testament admonition to 'drink water out of thine own cistern and running waters out of thine own well'. It would be fascinating to be able to understand the bizarre process by which Haigh's twisted mind shaped this thought to cause him to start drinking his own urine and blood.

Yes, this religious vampire's first taste of human blood was that of his own. He was in an automobile crash in which he suffered a scalp wound that bled profusely. The blood flowed down his face and into his mouth, thereby creating a subsequent thirst that would lead him to the gallows.

Perhaps it was the wound's accompanying blow to the head that had somehow deepened Haigh's psychosis.

Shortly after the incident, he had a dream that he interpreted to mean that his religious fervour had so sapped his strength that he could only restore his energies by the regular consumption of fresh human blood.

In keeping with the religious trend of his illness, Haigh evolved a ritual. First he would sever the jugular vein of his victim, then he would carefully draw off the blood, a glassful at a time. The actual drinking of the vital fluid was observed with great ceremony. Haigh later became convinced that his faith could only be sustained by the sacrifice of others and by the drinking of their blood.

After his arrest, Haigh revealed that he had been seduced by a homosexual member of a religious sect prior to the development of his desire to indulge in urine and blood. Some theorists have wondered if feelings of guilt arising from his homosexual experiences drove the impressionable Haigh to offer such terrible propitiation. Or, perhaps, Haigh may have mistaken the intoxication he reportedly felt from blood drinking for the 'high' that comes from religious ecstasy.

As fascinating as such theories may be as attempts to cast further light on vampirism, they will never be answered in the case of John Haigh, for his further testimonies became increasingly muddled until he was delivered to the hangman in August 1949.

On 30 October 1981 James P. Riva II was convicted in Brockton, Massachusetts, of murdering his grandmother and drinking her blood from the bullet holes. 'Voices' had told James that he was a vampire and that he must feast on human blood.

Serial killer Ted Bundy bit his victims and admitted that he felt like a vampire.

David ('Son of Sam') Berkowitz not only took his orders from a demonic dog, but claimed that he had been poisoned by bloodsucking demons.

*

Dr Stephen Kaplan, Director of the Vampire Research Center in New York, has been keeping tabs on real vampires since 1972. His current census estimates that there are at least five hundred known vampires worldwide who embark on nocturnal forays to obtain human blood.

According to the Vampire Research Center's 1989 census, the average male vampire appears to be about twenty-six years old, has brown eyes and hair, is five foot ten, and weighs 170 lbs. The average female vampire appears to be about twenty-three years old, has brown eyes and black hair, is five foot six, and weighs 120 lbs.

Dr Kaplan divides the creatures of the night into three basic categories:

1. Fetishists erotically attracted to blood
2. Vampire imitators who adopt the traditional trappings of cape, coffin, and Carpathian mannerisms in search of powers of domination, immortality, sensuality, and charisma
3. True vampires – men and women who have a physical addiction to blood, drink it, believe it will prolong their lives, and experience sexual satisfaction through the blood-drinking ritual.

Some true vampires murder their victims, Dr Kaplan states, but most find slightly more socially acceptable ways to satisfy their hunger for human blood.

One vampire works as a technician in a hospital. He simply takes blood from the hospital storage unit whenever he needs it. Although this man is supposedly well over sixty, he passes for a man in his early twenties.

A forty-year-old vampire in Arizona still looks like a teenager and hangs out around universities. He lures college girls into the desert and mesmerizes them while he sips their blood.

An attractive blonde, nearly seventy, who appears to be in her vigorous twenties, exchanges sexual favours for blood. Her willing victims allow her to use a scalpel to make incisions in their flesh so that she might drink their blood.

The vampire, the restless soul of the dead that must attach itself to the creatures on whose blood it feeds in order to sustain its 'life', is highly suggestive of the pathologically immature, dependent personality, who cannot fend for himself in the business of living, but must attach himself to a more productive personality in order to survive. Such individuals nearly always subconsciously desire to return to the condition of complete dependence characteristic of the prenatal state.

Psychoanalysts usually disclose that in extreme cases the grave comes to symbolize the womb. The vampire's return to his grave or coffin with each dawn's light suggests such a state of mind. The vampire's fangs are clearly phallic symbols, both in form and in function. The vampire's predilection for his relatives resembles the incestuous craving of the deviate, a form of infantile sexuality, as further symbolized by the vampire's relish for the young.

The desire to suck blood is itself significant. Psychologists say that any neurotic act involving this activity is a sign of mother-fixation.

A stake through the heart to kill a vampire is strongly suggestive of fear and connected hatred of the father figure.

It appears, therefore, that the true lair of the vampire must be sought in the hidden and forgotten areas of the human mind and that the terrible hunger of real-life vampires must be understood in the light of the frustration and misdirection of the most basic of human needs: the need to love and to reproduce one's own kind.

THE WEREWOLF OF SAN FRANCISCO

William Johnston, alias H. Meyers, alias Harry Gordon – the sadistic killer of three women – did not claw or bite his victims to death, but he earned his nickname fairly and viciously with a straight razor. Like London's infamous Jack the Ripper, Johnston chose prostitutes for his victims.

On the night of 6 April 1935, Betty Coffin turned a corner and started to walk down San Francisco's Market Street. As she passed under the streetlamp, she glanced at her wristwatch. It was 2:30 a.m., and her feet hurt. She had covered a lot of concrete during the last three hours and was about to call it a night.

Then she saw him.

It was too late to play coy games or to beat around the bush. She walked right up to the heavy-set, slightly drunk man, who was dressed like a seaman, and propositioned him.

'Sailor, do you know a nice quiet place where a girl can get some rest?'

Fifteen minutes later, Betty Coffin stood sleepily by as her client scribbled on a registration card in a cheap waterfront hotel.

A minute later, 'Mr and Mrs Harry Meyers' started up the stairs to their room. The night clerk barely noticed that the couple's only luggage was a bottle of whiskey and a little box that protruded from Meyers's pocket.

Two hours later Meyers came down alone. 'Where can I get a beer and a sandwich?' he half-spoke, half-yawned to the night clerk.

The clerk told him that there was a place on the corner. 'Just turn left after you go out the door.'

At eight o'clock the next morning a chambermaid entered the Meyers's room using a pass-key. She placed her broom against the wall and started to open a window. Then she saw the sprawled figure on the bed. Her screams brought the manager from downstairs.

The nude body of Betty Coffin lay on the blood-soaked sheets. Her face had been beaten savagely. Her mouth was taped shut.

The corpse was ripped open again and again with gaping wounds in regular patterns, as if she had been raked over and over by the claws of a wild beast. Blood-stained fragments of clothing were strewn about the room.

The dead girl had not been sexually assaulted – at least not in the normal way.

Inspector Allan McGinn of the San Francisco Police was quoted as saying, 'The man who does a job like this is the type that strikes again and again. He doesn't stop at one murder. It just whets his appetite for more.'

Newspapers blared stories of the werewolf's brutal and bloody savagery, but the most arduous of policework failed to turn up any clue of the killer.

Although five years passed without another werewolf murder, Inspector McGinn had been correct about the sadistic human monster working according to some inner cycle of blood lust. On 25 June 1940 the moon was right for the San Francisco werewolf to strike again.

The body of Mrs Irene Chandler was found in another waterfront hotel in the same condition as that of Betty Coffin. Official causes of death were listed as strangulation and loss of blood, but the corpse bore the same terrible beastlike slashings. Mrs Chandler was known to the police as a 'seagull', a streetwalker who catered to seafaring men. This time the werewolf had left his claws behind – a rusty, bloodstained razor.

Time was running out for the werewolf killer. The Sailors' Union of the Pacific supplied the police with a picture of a man whom they felt fit the murderer's description.

On 8 July 1940 a San Francisco detective confronted Harry W. Gordon at a sailors' union meeting. Gordon was a big blond man and the manner in which he had mutilated the two women indicated that he was bestial, cruel, and most likely a psychopath. The detective braced himself for a struggle.

Keeping his voice level, quiet, hoping to avert violence and to defuse the situation, the detective told Gordon that the police wanted to talk to him at headquarters.

Amazingly, the brute who had so hideously carved up two women slumped his shoulders and offered no resistance as he was taken to jail. After intense questioning, he broke down.

'I'll tell you everything. I'm glad to get it over with,' he said, confessing to the murders of Betty Coffin and Irene Chandler.

The officers were not prepared for Gordon's next confession: 'And I killed my first wife in New York, too!'

On 5 September 1941, Harry W. Gordon took his last breath in San Quentin's lethal gas chamber. The werewolf's savage hunger was quieted at last.

MAN WHO CLAIMED TO BE 'EVIL UNDEAD' IS HACKED TO PIECES BY FEARFUL VAMPIRE KILLER

The man who had found the pools of blood in the corridor and in the parking lot of the Ocean Breeze Apartments on 20 April 1986 was waiting at the front entrance of the apartments for the two patrol officers from the Virginia Beach, Virginia, Police Department.

The trail of blood led up the stairs to Apartment 348. A volunteered pass-key from the manager turned the lock, and the opened door released the sickening odour of decaying flesh. Fighting back their nausea and fearing the worst, the officers found a grisly assortment of body parts heaped in a pool of blood in the middle of the apartment floor.

Later, after the proper search warrant had been obtained,

investigating officers Sergeant Brian Kroft and Detective Tom Parks carefully examined the apartment with lab technicians. The place had been trashed, and there were unmistakable signs of a desperate struggle in the living room. Chunks of flesh and viscera, quite likely human, were dispatched to the state crime lab for the definitive analysis.

The investigators learned that the apartment had been rented by Marty Hughes, a husky middle-aged carpenter with a receding hairline and a thick moustache. The manager described Hughes as a model tenant.

On site at the construction company where Hughes had worked, the foreman depicted the carpenter as one of his best men. He had known something was wrong when Marty did not show up on the job without calling.

Although the man worked as a labourer in construction, the police investigators soon discovered that Marty Hughes had highbrow tastes that seemed to be in marked contrast to his blue-collar background. The man was not only an expert on the Civil War, but he also taught Gaelic, the ancient Celtic language of Ireland and certain Highland Scottish regions. In addition, Hughes took great delight in playing the bagpipes and the bluegrass mandolin.

Lieutenant Donald Hagen was finding it increasingly difficult to ascertain why anyone would kill a man that everyone seemed to like. What could the motive possibly be for such a bloody murder?

Learning that Hughes had lived in Boston, Massachusetts, Hagen assigned Sergeant Kroft to check out the murder victim's connections in that area. Once again it was determined that Hughes left nothing but friends behind wherever he travelled.

But later telephone calls provided the sergeant with an astonishing bit of information. According to certain of Hughes' relatives, the husky Celtic scholar, musician, historian, and contemporary Renaissance Man, also believed himself to be a vampire.

Lieutenant Hagen was not in the mood for jokes about

Dracula and Barnabas Collins. 'You don't mean like those vampires in the horror movies, do you, Sergeant?'

Kroft explained that Hughes was diagnosed as suffering from a rare and very peculiar kind of blood disease that made him develop vampirelike symptoms. 'It's called "porphyria", Lieutenant. Its victims are overly sensitive to sunlight and have an aversion to garlic – just like the vampires in the movies. In addition, the disease causes the person's gums to recede, making it look like he or she has fangs.'

The lieutenant wondered aloud if those bloody hunks of human flesh and organs that were left in the apartment could be the grisly remains of one of Hughes' victims? Had the man slipped over the edge and convinced himself that he truly was a creature of the night who must sustain himself on human blood?

On the other hand, the gory remains could be those of Hughes himself.

Sergeant Kroft noted that Hughes had been receiving injections from a medical doctor to 'pep up his blood' against the rare disease.

'Then let's have the medical examiner contact Hughes' doctor and find out what the exact medication was,' Lieutenant Hagen suggested. 'If Hughes is our chopped-up victim, there might be some traces of the drug in the body parts we took from the apartment.'

By the next day, the investigators had received their answer: traces of the drug heme, used to relieve those afflicted with porphyria, were detected in the human organs left in Hughes' apartment.

The police now had an identity for their gruesome pile of body parts. The next steps were to determine a motive and a murder suspect.

The only meagre clues that the investigators had were a few unidentified fingerprints on a beer bottle and the smudged impressions of bloody tennis shoes that led away from Hughes' apartment. Lab technicians stated that the small size of the shoes indicated that they had been worn by someone weighing around 130 lbs.

'It's a small shoe size, like a kid would wear,' they theorized. 'It would be hard to imagine such a little guy demolishing a husky, 200 lb carpenter.'

Police investigators were nearly out of leads when a sixteen-year-old girl and her seventeen-year-old boyfriend came forward with a startling story. They knew the murderer of Marty Hughes to be Dean Bolan, because he had told them so.

The police got lucky. Bolan had talked about the murder to other friends.

'I thought Dean was kidding,' another witness, who insisted upon anonymity, admitted to the police. 'He called me on the night of April twenty-third, yelling about how he had killed someone. He said his clothes were all bloody and everything. He asked if he could bring the body over and burn it up in my stove!'

'I thought he was nuts, completely insane,' the witness continued. 'I did set some clothes out for him, though. I mean, he kept screaming that he was covered from head to toe with blood.'

Providing a change of clothes for Bolan could make the witness an accessory to murder, but the police let it go. They wanted to know what Bolan looked like.

'He's a quiet little guy,' the witness said. 'He's only about five foot four. Can't weigh over 130 lbs or so.'

Police investigators later determined that Dean Bolan tipped the scales at only 120 lbs, but fear of the 'Evil Undead' had granted him superhuman strength on that terrible night of 23 April.

The remarkable details of Marty Hughes' death were learned during the sensational 'Vampire Murder Trial' that began at the Circuit Courthouse in January 1987. According to defence attorney Peter Gaines, Bolan had killed Hughes in self-defence.

Hughes, according to the defence, appeared affable and agreeable only to those who did not know him well. The big carpenter had a Jekyll-and-Hyde twist to his personality.

What is more, he regularly performed occult rituals to summon spirits from the dead.

The two men had met on a construction job two years earlier, and they had kept in touch. They were, the small man insisted, friends.

Bolan testified that the fateful evening in April had begun innocently enough in Hughes' apartment. After they had shared a pizza and a few beers, Hughes had stood up and begun dancing in a circle. 'I am a vampire. I am evil. I am a vampire,' he chanted over and over.

Bolan stated that he knew about the porphyria, the 'vampire's disease', and he assumed that his friend was just joking around, making light of his affliction.

But then Hughes presented his guest with a most intriguing offer. 'You can have your pick of any one of three evil spirits,' Marty said to Dean. 'I will allow you to make contact with the spirit of Billy the Kid . . . Adolf Hitler . . . or Jack the Ripper. Choose one. Tell me quick! Which one do you want?'

Still believing his friend to be joking, Bolan chose the spirit of Jack the Ripper.

Hughes pulled a book off his cluttered shelves. He began reading aloud in eerie-sounding Gaelic phrases. He made a few peculiar movements, then began to shout that he had become possessed by an evil spirit. 'I am evil. I am evil. I am evil,' he chanted.

Bolan testified that he now became very uneasy. Hughes no longer sounded as though he might be teasing or joking around.

Everything took on a sharp and jagged edge when Hughes told Bolan that the evil spirit was communicating with him, giving him orders. 'The evil spirit commands that I must kill you!' Marty told Dean.

Bolan's eyes bulged in horror when he saw his friend moving toward him with a maniacal gleam in his eyes and a wicked knife in his hand. The two men fought; Hughes tripped and fell on the blade.

Although his defence attorney maintained the storyline of self-defence, neither Bolan nor his lawyer offered a really sound explanation to satisfy the question of why he had not simply called the police and told them the facts of his friend's death. Instead, they confessed to the jury, Dean panicked and decided that he must somehow get rid of Hughes' body.

Since the victim weighed well over 200 lbs, he was too heavy for Bolan to lift. He couldn't just leave the corpse there in the apartment. It would be impossible to drag it down the stairs without being detected.

Frightened. Confused. What was there left for him to do?

'Because there was no way to dispose of the body as it was,' defence attorney Gaines told a stunned and disgusted jury, 'he did the unimaginable. He cut the body in half.'

Bolan and his attorney admitted that the concept of dismemberment may sound loathsome and insane to the rational mind, but it seemed the best idea at the time. Setting to work on his friend's body with a hacksaw, stuffing body parts into foot lockers and garbage bags, all the gore seemed logical in the context of the madness of the evening.

After six hours in deliberation, the jury reached a verdict that found Dean Bolan guilty of second-degree murder. The fearful vampire killer who swore that Marty Hughes became truly possessed by an evil spirit after the chanting of ancient Celtic ritual is currently serving his twenty-year term in prison.

CHAPTER SEVENTEEN

SUICIDE AND SELF-INFLICTED INJURIES

WIFE OF RADIO TALK SHOW HOST KILLS HERSELF AFTER CALLING IN HER PROBLEM

There must have been *something* familiar about the voice of the woman who called New Orleans radio talk show host Ron Hunter to complain about her marital problems.

On Wednesday 20 June 1990, Hunter, fifty-one, was taking calls on his programme with his guest, Dr Judith Kuriansky, a sex therapist, when a female telephoned to detail a marriage in which she and her spouse were drifting apart.

The therapist advised the caller that it would be best if she and her husband sought professional counselling.

The caller said that they had already tried that approach to their problems, then added, 'My husband nixed that idea after the first or second session.'

Narrowing the focus of the dilemma and speaking frankly, Dr Kuriansky said, 'You may have to give him a real big ultimatum. You may have to push him off his chair and make him say, "Oh, my God, I don't want to lose you." '

The radio audience was then astonished to hear the woman caller retort, 'Well, why don't *you* push him off the chair? He's sitting two feet from you.'

Ron and Marilou 'Bunny' Hunter, thirty-two, married in 1980 and had two children. If the talk show host had not been fully aware of his wife's emotional concern over the status of their marriage, he received the definitive word together with his listeners.

Thursday night, ten hours after Marilou had dramatically telephoned Ron's talk show to air her distress, she shot herself in the chest as she lay beside her sleeping husband.

Hunter told police that he had been awakened by a 'loud pop' at about 2:00 a.m. When he turned on a light, he was startled to see blood on the wall. His .38-calibre pistol lay next to Marilou.

New Orleans police listed the death as unclassified, pending further investigation.

THE UNKINDEST CRIME OF ALL – WHEN YOUR RIGHT HAND DOESN'T KNOW YOUR LEFT HAND IS STRANGLING YOU

According to certain medical experts, thousands of people suffer from a bizarre disorder called 'alien hand syndrome', which causes one of their own hands to act as if it had a mind of its own.

An assistant professor of physiology and physical medicine rehabilitation at Temple University said that patients who have this strange ailment can discover their 'alien hand' pulling their hair from their scalp, clawing their flesh bloody, and even strangling themselves to death. It is as if the 'alien hand' were truly being controlled by another person.

Medical researchers have speculated that the bizarre malady may be caused by a stroke that damages a part of the brain that controls hand movements. 'Alien hand syndrome' may strike both men and women, and most victims are in their fifties or older.

'We believe that "alien hand syndrome" hits about one in a thousand stroke victims, and that there are several thousand new cases each year in the United States,' a doctor commented. 'Fortunately, the problem clears itself up in almost all cases within six months to a year, because the brain makes new connections and in effect heals itself.'

FEARFUL OF GIRLFRIEND'S WRATH, MAN HAS HIMSELF SHOT TO PROVIDE ALIBI FOR BEING LATE

Like most men, Eddie Hernandez would rather look eye-to-eye with a mean junkyard dog than face an icy stare from his girlfriend when he is late. And that day in June 1990, he was very late picking up Juanita from her doctor's office. After all, she would remind him, it was with his child that she was pregnant.

He had been late before – too often before. This time Juanita would kill him. If she had a gun, she would shoot him.

That was when the twenty-year-old Santa Cruz man came up with a scheme that he thought would surely get him off the hook with Juanita. He asked his friend Luis to shoot him in the shoulder.

'No way, man,' Luis protested. 'Are you nuts? You are two sandwiches short of a picnic!'

Eddie desperately explained the problem. Nothing serious. You know, just a flesh wound. 'I need a wound just big enough to tell Juanita that I was held up by robbers. That way she can't be mad at me for being late picking her up at the doctor's office.'

Luis at last weakened to his friend's pleadings, but in order to make the distasteful job easier for him, he closed his eyes to miss all the bloodshed. The 'slight flesh wound' suddenly became a hole that went completely through Eddie's shoulder and back.

Hernandez blinked his eyes in astonishment, screamed at the blood that gushed from the ragged puncture in his shoulder, and went into shock.

Some other friends of Hernandez decided that Luis had done enough to help Eddie, so they rushed him to a hospital. During his periods of painful consciousness, Hernandez realized that if he played it cool, he could still pull off the perfect alibi. The police would soon be informed of a gunshot wound, and they would arrive to question him.

Eddie's first story of a robbery fell flat. The cops didn't believe the second phoney encounter, either; and their cold, icy stares were almost as bad as Juanita's.

It finally occurred to Eddie that he had no escape routes left open to him. He had no choice other than to tell the police the whole wild and wacky truth.

Once the police officers found that the strange tale of one man's desperate lengths to avoid his girlfriend's wrath checked out, they encouraged him to tell Juanita the truth just as he had presented it to them.

Eddie still dreaded such a disclosure. By now Juanita would really be furious. She had waited at the doctor's office for hours. Maybe she would buy the story of the robbers even if the police had not.

That was when Detective Bill Squires reminded him that honesty was the best policy. 'Remember,' he advised Hernandez, 'she's going to read all about it in the papers tomorrow, anyway.'

HATE-FILLED FATHER KILLS HIMSELF, FRAMES HIS SON FOR MURDER

The foul deed of murder skilfully rearranged in order to look like suicide is a staple plot line of mystery fiction. But the act of suicide committed in order to frame an innocent man for murder is so bizarre that it could only happen in real life.

In 1989 in Asenby, England, a father was so perversely filled with hatred that he manipulated his own grisly suicide in such a way that his despised son would be charged with murder.

Jeffrey Barley would be the first to admit that he and his father had never really got along. In fact, Jeffrey left home at the age of sixteen and had very little contact with his father until he returned in 1988 at the age of forty-eight.

Jeffrey had done quite well as an oil company executive, and when he had to undergo two medical operations, his mother invited him to the family home to recuperate. Jeffrey decided to accept the kind offer, and he made plans to retire because of his disability.

Victor Barley, eighty-one, began a steady campaign of vicious verbal attacks almost the very day that their convalescing son moved home. Jeffrey had hoped that the passage of so many years had tempered his father's nearly pathological disdain for him, but it was immediately apparent that the elder Barley had carefully kept the fires of hatred well stoked in the thirty-two years that they had been apart.

Victor had always been a tyrant who had to have everything his own way. In addition, he cherished the belief that things had been so much better in the 'good old days'. So fanatically was he devoted to this nostalgic concept of the past that he did not allow a television set or even a telephone in the house.

It took no time at all to perceive that the relationship between father and son was just as rocky and rough as it had always been. Jeffrey was the only one who had ever stood up to the grumpy, old-fashioned dictator, and after one particularly noisy altercation, Victor became so enraged that he picked up Jeffrey's television set and hurled it out a window.

The two men finally came to blows one day when Victor began to ridicule and insult Jeffrey's mother. His father continued the unmerciful attack in spite of Jeffrey warning him to leave Mum alone.

At last the younger man could no longer tolerate the distasteful scene of his father abusing his mother, so he walked over to Victor and shoved him down into a chair. 'Stop it!' Jeffrey warned him. 'Keep a civil tongue in your head and stop picking on Mother.'

Jeffrey was not prepared for what next transpired. With surprising agility, his father jumped from the chair, seized a poker from the fireplace, and struck him.

Jeffrey recoiled from the pain of the cruel blow, and while he reeled across the room, his father ran from the house.

Both Jeffrey and his mother were astonished when they learned that Victor had gone next door to the neighbours to call the police. While mother and son attempted to explain the true cause of the fight, Victor shouted down all efforts to establish reason with his shouts that Jeffrey had struck him and had threatened him with great bodily harm.

Fearing for his mother's safety, Jeffrey resolved to remain in the house – even though Victor had instructed his attorney to take out an injunction barring him from the family home. The still-enraged elder Barley informed his attorney that Jeffrey had made murderous threats against his physical person.

A few weeks later, on 22 August, 1989 while Mrs Barley was out of the house, Jeffrey heard an odd noise from his parents' bedroom. Knowing that his father had retired, he went to investigate. When he entered the room, he could see that Dad was lying in bed, wearing both the top and the bottoms of his pyjamas.

Jeffrey found this strange, since his father never wore a pyjama top in the summer, always complaining that it was too warm for him. Even stranger, of course, was the widening pool of blood that issued from his father's chest. A crumpled handkerchief lay beside the man, as if it were somehow intended to soak up the vital fluid.

Although the only source of illumination issued from a dim light bulb in the hallway, it was clear to see that Victor had stabbed himself in the chest. Somehow, though, he had managed to pull the death weapon clear of his flesh before he died.

The doctor proved unnecessary. Victor Barley was dead.

Jeffrey said that it was only after the undertakers had come to remove his father's body that he saw the kitchen knife that lay on the darkened bedroom floor. He decided to move it out of sight when he heard his mother returning home. He didn't want her to see the tool that her husband had used to end his life.

Moving the knife, of course, was Jeffrey Barley's big mistake. Carelessly, he placed his fingerprints all over the blade and the handle. And it did not take the police laboratory long to find perfect prints on a knife that had been suddenly transformed into 'the murder weapon'.

Jeffrey Barley was grilled by the police for ten hours before he was formally charged with the murder of his father. He protested that the authorities had to be joking. He was innocent. As much as he was tired of the old man's abuse, he surely would not kill his own father.

Jeffrey had eleven months to understand that the cruel joke was on him. As he sat behind bars in a tiny cell awaiting his trial, he came at last to realize that he had fallen victim to his father's evil plan to work a terrible revenge on him from beyond the grave. Victor Barley had killed himself and had managed to make it look like murder so that his son would rot in prison for the rest of his life.

Jeffrey knew that he was innocent and that he had been alone in the house with his father at the time of his death. As incredible as it might seem to any sane and rational person, Jeffrey theorized that his father had wrapped a handkerchief around the handle of the knife to keep his own fingerprints from the weapon.

Victor Barley had dressed in his complete pyjama outfit to look 'respectable' when the undertakers came. Then he had lain down on the bed, plunged the knife into his own heart and with his last bit of strength, pulled out the blade and thrown it on the floor. With his stabbed body on the bed and the knife on the floor, it would look as though he had been murdered. And old Victor had probably been counting on Jeffrey to be so naïve as to pick up the 'murder weapon' and obligingly place his fingerprints all over the handle, thus implicating himself as the murderer.

Jeffrey knew then why Victor Barley had provoked the fight that day when he had abused his mother and struck him with the fireplace poker. The old man had wanted it on record that the police had responded to a call in which his son had 'threatened' him.

Then there was also the matter of the lawyer taking out an injunction to kick Jeffrey out of the house. Victor Barley had been cleverly masterminding a scenario in which it would appear to investigators that his son wanted to kill him.

Jeffrey realized that his interpretation of the evidence of his father's death would probably sound totally ridiculous to the jury. They would more than likely ascribe such a wild and wayout theory to the ravings of a desperate man who would soon be sentenced to spend the rest of his days behind bars.

But Victor Barley, the wicked wizard of revenge, had made one serious mistake in his sinister machinations: he changed his will only five days before his death.

'It was as if he knew he was going to die very soon,'

Jeffrey argued in court in July 1990. 'How could my father have known so precisely when he was going to die – unless he was planning to kill himself?'

Nearly a year in jail had given Jeffrey Barley a lot of time to practise his argument, and he methodically presented his interpretation of the elaborate stages of development in his father's wickedly ingenious plan.

After a five-day trial, the jury at last announced their verdict of 'not guilty'. Victor Barley had managed to put his son through a living hell, but Jeffrey had won the final round.

As the verdict was being read, those nearest Jeffrey Barley saw him look up towards the ceiling of the court and heard his hoarse whisper of victory: 'Ha! I finally beat you, Dad!'

CHAPTER EIGHTEEN

VANDALISM

THREE-YEAR-OLD PLACED UNDER ARREST FOR MOVING NEIGHBOURS' PINK PLASTIC FLAMINGOS

The day had certainly begun quietly and innocently enough. Mrs Margit Salgado was reading to her four children as they sat outside their home in Ridge Manor, Florida, on 14 May 1990.

As his mother read, three-year-old Tony wandered across the street and picked up two pink plastic flamingos from a neighbour's lawn. When he returned with his newly claimed toys, Mrs Salgado ordered two of her older children to return the flamingos to Connie Vann's lawn and to replace them exactly where they had stood before Tony 'borrowed' them.

After a little while, when the lawn decorations were replaced, she personally apologized to Mrs Vann for Tony's childish invasion of her lawn.

Two hours later, an astonished Margit Salgado opened her front door to Deputy Mack Schroeder of the Hernando County Sheriff's Office. Deputy Schroeder proceeded to accuse her of not having any control over her children. A brief discussion with three-year-old Tony was all the deputy needed to conclude that the child could not determine right from wrong.

The law-enforcement officer informed Mrs Salgado that Tony would have to be further evaluated by the Florida

Department of Health and Rehabilitative Services (HRS), the state's official child-protection agency. In the mean time, he stated ominously, Tony must be placed under house arrest.

Mrs Salgado said that she did not understand what it meant to be placed under house arrest.

Deputy Schroeder coldly answered that it was the same as being legally arrested, except that Tony would be placed in her custody and could not leave the house.

After the officer left, Mrs Salgado was in tears. She had tried to explain that she and her children were not looking for trouble and that she would promise to keep Tony out of the Vanns' yard, but her pleas had been to no avail. Her baby, three-year-old Tony, had been placed under house arrest.

And Tony stayed under house arrest for the next two weeks. Mrs Salgado kept her three-year-old jailbird inside the house nearly twenty-four hours a day, anxiously awaiting word from HRS.

Finally, after the weeks of confinement had passed, a local journalist arrived at the Salgado home to inform the family that the charges against Tony had been dropped.

Later that same day, Sheriff Thomas Mylander of Hernando County called to apologize to Mr and Mrs Salgado. Sheriff Mylander said that he understood their outrage, and he emphasized that his office did not condone the actions of Deputy Schroeder.

Connie Vann, who had started it all by telephoning the local sheriff's department after the three-year-old tot had moved her lawn ornaments, explained that she had not expected such a 'sledgehammer reaction' from the law. She had only wanted an officer to speak to Mrs Salgado about 'a neighbourhood problem'. She had not intended little Tony to be arrested.

Sergeant Frank Bierwiler admitted that it had all been a very bad scene. 'We're not in the habit of arresting toddlers,' he said.

WHO STOLE THE BONES OF EDGAR ALLAN POE?

If the ghost of Edgar Allan Poe walks at midnight, it no doubt chortles gleefully as it surveys the macabre graveyard in which its earthly remains were interred. The things that have happened to the Westminster Presbyterian church cemetery in downtown Baltimore comprise a horror story that is the equal of any conceived in the imagination of that tormented genius of American letters. And it is exceedingly appropriate that a book about strange, bizarre, and eerie crimes is able to include a misadventure of the skeletal remains of the very patron saint of weird crime.

Poe died, either drunk or drugged, on a bleak October day in 1849. Two days later he was laid to rest next to the grave of his illustrious grandfather, Major David Poe, a Revolutionary War hero. Because of a most inefficient custom of the day, which seemed to care not one whit for the concerns of posterity, the younger Poe's grave was left unmarked in the family plot.

Today a monument marks the alleged site of the author's grave, but there is ample reason to doubt whether the bones, which so many tourists come annually to revere, are really those of Edgar Allan Poe.

In 1875, after the author had achieved posthumous fame, what were believed to be his remains were disinterred and shifted. It should have been relatively easy at that date to determine just whose bones were whose, except for one annoying fact: vandals had long since made off with the major's gravestone. When what may have been Edgar's remains were shifted, someone else's bones had to be similarly disturbed and moved about, and in the process of all this grave swapping, no one can now say just exactly whose grave is whose.

When will all this confusion be solved? Poe's raven would undoubtedly quote us the answer: 'Nevermore!'

To add another disturbing element to the plot of our little horror story, it is quite possible that Poe's remains no longer rest in the cemetery at all. It is a well-known, albeit rather grisly, fact, that medical students of the day were often forced to empty graves in order to secure fresh cadavers for the anatomy class dissecting table. In Baltimore, Westminster Cemetery seemed to bear the brunt of such ghoulish raids.

A persistent legend has it that one class of medical students deliberately set out to exhume the remains of Edgar Allan Poe. According to one version of the account, this was done for pure ghoulish delight – a chance to romp with the bones of the master of horror and terror. A more charitable rendering of the legend has the budding doctors seeking better to understand whatever it was that gave Poe his unique genius.

Whether such a midnight foray occurred specifically to steal the bones of Edgar Allan Poe, the grim fact remains that on one violent night the irate residents of the area caught some medical students at their macabre 'homework' and promptly hanged one of them on the corner of Baltimore and Greene Streets as a dramatic sort of object lesson.

In the 1920s, the neighbourhood was well into a process of decay that was steadily transforming the area from a fashionable residential district into a slum. And in the graveyard strange, bizarre things began happening at night.

A succession of young men committed suicide by climbing to the top of the church steeple, winding the bell rope around their necks and jumping to their deaths by hanging. An eerie tolling of the bell, set into clanging motion by the weight of a fresh corpse on the rope, would announce another suicide to the residents of the area.

Dr Bruce McDonald, who served the Westminster Presbyterian church as pastor until 1959, recalled the day in 1929 when he had his first look at the cemetery. 'I found all the tombs in the graveyard open and children running about the street with skulls on broomsticks.'

Youngsters in the area had, it seemed, discovered the cemetery to be a most fascinating playground and had begun to break into the vaults to make off with a skull, a bone, or even, in some instances, a complete skeleton.

Dr McDonald also remembered the day on which a crypt was opened to accept a new body and the astonished caretaker discovered that another body had already taken its place. Police concluded that the decomposing corpse was that of a murder victim who had been locked into the vault while still alive. Shades of Poe's short stories 'The Premature Burial' and 'The Cask of Amontillado'!

Periodic efforts to raise money to rehabilitate the cemetery end in repeated failures. However, tourists who make the pilgrimage to Poe's 'grave' seem to find it quite appropriate that the resting place of the old master of the macabre should be overgrown with weeds, cluttered with toppled gravestones, and eerie with the creaking hinges of open vault doors. No doubt Edgar would have been delighted.

GALLERY OF THE WILD, THE WEIRD AND THE EVIL

Real-life vampires who drink human blood and possess eternal youth . . . teenagers who sacrifice a young girl on Satan's altar . . . the beautiful seductress whose love is the kiss of death . . . the intruder who is beaten within an inch of his life by enraged nuns . . . the Trappist monks who become Holymen from Hell . . . the judge who rules that a man *can* be in two places at a time . . .

Get ready to meet these men, women, children and fiends in human form. You'll be the star witness to their twisted deeds and startling fates in the book that proves that crime pays off in stranger ways than you've ever imagined.